Pattern Recognition Algorithms for Symbol Strings

Dissertation

der Fakultät für Informations- und Kognitionswissenschaften
der Eberhard-Karls-Universität Tübingen
zur Erlangung des Grades eines
Doktors der Naturwissenschaften
(Dr. rer. nat.)

vorgelegt von
Dipl.-Ing. Igor Fischer
aus Zagreb

Tübingen
2003

Bibliografische Information Der Deutschen Bibliothek

Die Deutsche Bibliothek verzeichnet diese Publikation in der Deutschen
Nationalbibliografie; detaillierte bibliografische Daten sind im Internet über
http://dnb.ddb.de abrufbar.

ISBN 3-8325-0557-1

Logos Verlag Berlin
Comeniushof, Gubener Str. 47,
10243 Berlin
Tel.: +49 030 42 85 10 90
Fax: +49 030 42 85 10 92
INTERNET: http://www.logos-verlag.de

Tag der mündlichen Qualifikation: 29.10.2003

Dekan:	Prof. Dr. Martin Hautzinger
1. Berichterstatter:	Prof. Dr. Andreas Zell
2. Berichterstatter:	Prof. Dr. Wolfgang Rosenstiel

Abstract

Traditionally, pattern recognition has been concerned mostly with numerical data, i.e. vectors of real-valued features. Less often, symbolic representations of data have been used. A special category of data, symbol strings, have been neglected for a long time, partially because of a perceived lack of urgency and partially because of the high computational costs involved. Only recently, motivated by research in such diverse fields as speech recognition and computational molecular biology, symbols strings attracted more interest from the pattern recognition community.

Two large families of pattern recognition algorithms – those based on distance and those based on a kernel – can be applied to strings by defining a distance measure (and, in some cases, an average) or a kernel function on strings. String versions of self-organizing maps and LVQ have already been implemented in the context of speech recognition. However, they relied on feature distance, which has several drawbacks. Also, a number of kernels for strings are already known, but with a limited scope.

In this thesis, mathematically and biologically founded distance measures and averages, as well as kernels for strings are defined. Based on them, various classical algorithms for visualization, clustering, and classification are adapted for string data. The performance is tested on artificial and real-world data. It is shown that the algorithms can be applied on strings in the same way and with the same purpose as for numeric data. Beside the above mentioned, possible applications include marketing, user interface optimization, and behavioral sciences in general.

Kurzfassung

Mustererkennung befasst sich traditionell überwiegend mit numerischen Daten, also mit Vektoren von reellwertigen Merkmalen. Seltener wird eine symbolische Repräsentation verwendet. Eine spezielle Kategorie der Daten, nämlich Symbolketten (Strings), wurde lange Zeit vernachlässigt, teilweise wegen der scheinbar nicht vorhandenen Notwendigkeit und teilweise wegen des damit verbundenen hohen Rechenaufwands. Erst in jüngster Zeit, veranlasst durch die Forschung in unterschiedlichen Gebieten, wie Spracherkennung und Bioinformatik, weckten Symbolketten ein höheres Interesse unter den Forschern im Gebiet der Mustererkennung.

Zwei große Familien der Mustererkennungsalgorithmen – distanzbasierte und kernelbasierte – können auf Symbolketten angewandt werden, indem man ein Distanzmaß (und, in manchen Fällen, einen Mittelwert) oder eine Kernelfunktion für Symbolketten definiert. String-Varianten von selbstorganisierenden Karten und LVQ wurden bereits im Kontext von Spracherkennung implementiert. Sie basierten jedoch auf der *feature distance*, die verschiedene Nachteile hat. Auch zahlreiche Kernels für Strings sind schon bekannt, deren Anwendbarkeit ist jedoch auf bestimmte Bereiche begrenzt.

In dieser Dissertation werden mathematisch und biologisch begründete Distanzmaße und Mittelwerte, wie auch Kernels für Strings definiert. Darauf basierend werden verschiedene klassische Algorithmen für Datenvisualisierung, Klassifizierung und Clustering für Anwendungen an Strings adaptiert. Deren Güte wird auf künstlichen und natürlichen Datensätzen getestet. Es wird gezeigt, dass sich die Algorithmen auf dieselbe Art und mit derselben Zielsetzung wie für numerische Daten auch auf Strings anwenden lassen. Weitere mögliche Anwendungsbereiche, neben den oben erwähnten, schließen Marketing, Optimierung von Schnittstellen und Verhaltenswissenschaften im Allgemeinen ein.

Acknowledgements

My research and, consequently, this thesis would not have been possible without the help, support, constructive critic, advice, and much more from my friends, colleagues, students and parents. My greatest gratitude belongs to my Ph.D. supervisor, Professor Andreas Zell, who chairs the Department of Computer Architecture of the Wilhelm-Schickard-Institute for Informatics at the University of Tübingen. He has offered me a research position, granted me the freedom in research and always knew to direct my attention to the right questions. His suggestions and guidance have been highly valuable for my work. Thanks to his strategic planning and personal engagement the technical infrastructure at the department has allowed smooth and highly efficient research. And, last but not least, in his department he hosts numerous excellent researchers from different professional backgrounds, with whom I have often had very informative discussions and who have offered me different insights into problems. My thanks also go to Professor Wolfgang Rosenstiel, who kindly accepted the task of evaluating my thesis.

Of my colleagues, I am especially grateful to Jan Poland for his advice and suggestions, ranging from highly theoretical mathematics to practical hints and tips concerning MatLab and other software. He and Jutta Huhse were the first to critically read this thesis and made it better through their suggestions. With Holger Ulmer I had numerous discussions, both about pattern recognition and software design. Concerning design – software, and even more graphical – Simon Wiest has been of an indispensable help, knowing answers to all kinds of formatting problems. Fred Rapp has been a valuable source of information about neural networks, and he has drawn my attention to algorithms in computational molecular biology. Valuable tips, from biology to LaTeX formatting, have been provided by Markus Schwehm, and in the field of neural networks, as well as in numerous other questions, I had the assistance of Guo-Jian Cheng, Kosmas Knödler, and Clemens Jürgens. The latter have also significantly supported me in my everyday work with students, as have Badreddin Abolmaali and Ralf Tetzlaff.

Students Fabian Hennecke and Fabian Sinz have been of an enormous help in the implementation of the software framework used for experiments. In addition, Fabian Sinz compiled one of the data sets, and another I owe to my colleague Stephan Steigele.

Although not directly involved in the research, Claudia Walter, Kurt Langenbacher and Klaus Beyreuther made it possible by sustaining the department's organizational and technical infrastructure. They, as well as other colleagues who I cannot all name here, are also responsible for the pleasant working atmosphere. Finally, my thanks go to my father, who introduced me to computer science and whose remarks on artificial intelligence I began to understand only decades later, and to Hana, who patiently tolerated my long working hours.

iv

Contents

Chapter 1

Introduction

Much of the real-world data can – and indeed has to – be represented numerically: length, mass, pressure, temperature and so on are all real values. All kinds of sensory data are numerical in nature, and handling them as such is inevitable in the early stages of information processing. Nevertheless, in further stages, a numerical representation is in many cases not possible, or at least does not reflect the structure of the data in a natural way. A kind of symbolical representation might be desirable. This thesis is concerned with symbolic data structured in a special way, namely symbol strings.

A big family of data processing algorithms are the pattern recognition algorithms. They are usually applied with the purpose of obtaining the information about the processes which generate the data. This is achieved by looking for regularities in the data. Pattern recognition is often used in the early stages of research in many empirical sciences, from physics to behavioral science.

1.1 Motivation for this thesis

Traditionally, pattern recognition has been concerned mostly with numerical data, i.e. vectors of real-valued features. Less often, a symbolic representation of data has been used. A special category of data, the symbol strings, have been neglected for a long time, partially because of a perceived lack of urgency and partially because of the high computational cost involved. Only recently, motivated by research in such diverse fields like speech recognition and computational molecular biology, symbols strings acquired more interest in the pattern recognition community. This thesis investigates the applicability of various pattern recognition techniques on symbol string data and tries to bridge the gap between symbolical and statistical pattern recognition in this special field. Application areas are various: speech recognition, molecular biology, and social sciences, to name just a few.

1

As an example, let us consider the problem of speech recognition. The task is to correctly assign spoken words to the words in a dictionary available to the pattern recognition system, i.e. to classify spoken words. Just to make the example easier, let us assume that voice has already been preprocessed and segmented into phonemes. Then, each phoneme can be assigned a symbol, so that the input into the classifier is a continuous sequence of symbols – a symbol string. Due to noise, some phonemes can become distorted, not recognized at all, or other artifacts can appear, making the classification nontrivial. The classifier would have to use some kind of similarity criterion to decide which word from the dictionary is most likely to be the one corresponding to the sequence of phonemes.

A straightforward approach would be to assign normative pronunciations to all words in a dictionary, code them as strings using the same symbols as for the input data, and try to compare observed strings with those in the dictionary. The comparison, however, is bound to fail if it is not designed to be fault tolerant. Because of the above mentioned noise, strings produced from spoken words will seldom completely match the dictionary strings. Another issue is of determining normative pronunciation. It can be done by a human expert, but this bears the risk of being biased towards one specific pronunciation, considered "right" by the expert, and neglecting a variety of other, possibly more common pronunciations. It would be preferable to derive the normative, prototypical pronunciation automatically from a large set of spoken words. It can, of course, happen that some words have more than one "correct" pronunciation.

This simple example shows some of the issues being covered in this thesis. It should be noted that the thesis mainly investigates general principles of applying pattern recognition to strings. Descriptions of applications appear only to underline motivation or as explanatory examples. Many of them are concerned with issues from molecular biology, for two reasons: First, computational molecular biology is currently an area of intensive scientific research and applying statistical pattern recognition to it proves its practical relevance. The other reason lies in the complexity of problems in that field, which makes it a good and realistic testbed for algorithms.

1.2   An overview of pattern recognition

Pattern recognition is today recognized as a field inside computer science. It is related to many other research areas, like statistics, neural networks, artificial intelligence, data mining, and machine learning. Pattern recognition is normally not applied to raw data, but to features – a small number of highly informational parameters extracted from the data. Feature extraction is itself a large research field. For symbol strings, the features are the symbols.

Some authors consider pattern recognition a synonym for pattern classification, or as a common name for classification and clustering (see Duda et al., 2001, Friedman and Kandel, 1999). Others, like Bishop (1995), also include regression (function approximation or estimation) as a branch of pattern recognition. Which of the three we can apply in a particular case, depends on the information provided with the training set or, in other words, our knowledge about the data.

If a relationship between the features can be postulated, so that some can be estimated from the others, the former can be considered dependent variables and the latter independent. The relationship connecting the independent variables with the dependent is assumed to be unknown. If no such relationship can be postulated, all features are considered independent variables. Data consisting only of independent values are called *unlabeled*. Labeling is normally performed, more or less directly, by an expert: The dependent features are determined, for example, by measurements of process output for independent features, or by manually assigning the values.

Methods applicable to unlabeled data belong to the family of clustering algorithms. The purpose of clustering is to find out if the data form local groups, or clusters, characterized by an above-average degree of closeness (or similarity) between its members.

With dependent variables present, one can try to deduce the unknown relationship connecting them to the independent variables. The word "unknown" is to be taken conditionally here, for we need to make some assumptions about it, as will be shown later. The type of dependent variables determines the possible kinds of analysis. If they can be represented by a real-valued vector, we have a case for regression. Otherwise, if the dependent variables are inherently nominal – labels for classes –, the task is to discover a rule by which independent variables imply the class membership. Classification is often regarded as a special case of regression. To be useful in practice, both regression and classification algorithms have to fulfill one crucial requirement: the applicability of the results on new, unseen data or, in other words, the ability to generalize beyond the training set. For real-world applications, the discovered regularities are not interesting unless they can be used on new data, with unknown dependent values.

Current pattern recognition algorithms stem from many different fields, from statistics (Pearson, 1896, Fisher, 1936) to neurobiology (McCulloch and Pitts, 1943, Pitts and McCulloch, 1947, Hebb, 1949), and are included in standard computer science curricula (see, for example, Fischer and Zell, 2000c, Fischer et al., 2000). Some algorithms, most representative and suitable for symbol strings, are discussed in this thesis. In order to make the choice plausible, the following section takes a look at pattern recognition systems from the perspective of their properties.

1.3   Structure of pattern recognition systems

In a pattern recognition system, several components determine its performance:

1. Data model,
2. Learning algorithm,
3. Recall mechanism.

The data model is a simplified description of the "world" (usually called domain) in which the pattern recognition system is designed to operate. Depending on the system architecture, the model can be stored in different ways: as formulae, sets of rules, sample data, algorithms, and so on. Together, they will be referred to as the "system parameters".

Determining the parameters is the key task, and is performed by the learning algorithm. The number of possible parameter settings in a system can be very large, so that checking them all is not a realistic option. The learning algorithm should be designed to lead quickly to good settings, at least with a high probability, if not deterministically.

For a specific pattern recognizer, the system architecture is fixed and effectively limits the representation power of the system. If, for example, we decide to use linear regression, we abandon the possibility of discovering nonlinear (e.g. exponential, quadratic, etc.) dependencies in the data: the only system parameters that can be adapted are the slope and the displacement. This can become a problem if we start from wrong assumptions when analyzing the data. Then, even with the best learning algorithms and with the best data, the results we get will be far from correct.

Once the system has been trained, we wish to exploit the model it has built. In case of clustering, we want to know which clusters have been identified, their positions, boundaries etc. The recall (if we want to call it such) is therefore limited to providing these values and is independent of any data beyond the training samples. In classification and regression, the recall consists of applying the model on new data and predicting the correct output (class or function value) for them. It is usually a straightforward task in case of regression, but in pattern classification, recall methods might differ in the way how they solve ambiguities and inconsistencies which are likely to appear. For example, a model, applied on a previously unseen datum, might try to classify it into more than one class concurrently, or into none.

1.3.1   Data models

Knowledge representation in a pattern recognition system can vary between two extremes: global and local. In a global representation, every system parameter can potentially influence the output for any input datum. Such is the case in linear regression and for the perceptron.

In the case of a local representation, the parameters can be divided subsets so that only one of them always determines the output for the given input and all other parameters can be neglected. Here we have a set of local, non-overlapping functions, with always only one of them being active in recall. Splines, locally linear functions and nearest-neighbor classifiers are typical examples employing local models.

If the functions overlap, but never cover the entire input space, or if they are weighted in dependence of the input, the representation is somewhere between local and global. Radial-basis-function networks and the K-nearest-neighbors classifier belong to this category. Systems with a non-local representation are also said to distribute knowledge, for it is disperesed over many parameters. Knowledge distribution has gained much popularity through artificial neural networks.

Knowledge representation is a description of data or relationships between them in terms of their features. Regarding the required data properties, virtually all pattern recognition systems require either the scalar product or a distance measure to be defined. Architectures requiring both, like counterpropagation (Hecht-Nielsen, 1987), are rare exceptions. Support vector machines rely in essence on the scalar product, but in practice, a kernel function is used instead. Thus the categorization of the algorithms can be well performed based on the question if they require the data to be from a vector space or if already a metric space suffices. Perceptrons, for example, require the scalar product and are therfore used for numerical data. The nearest-neighbor classifier, as the name suggests, is an example of a distance-based system, as well as self-organizing maps[1].

For symbol strings – the objects this thesis is about – there is no scalar product defined, but it is possible to define distance measures, as well as kernel functions on them. For that reason, only distance- and kernel-based methods will be described in depth here.

1.3.2 Learning algorithms

In his book "Machine Learning", Mitchell (1997) offers the following definition of learning:

> A computer program is said to **learn** from experience E with respect to some class of task T and performance measure P, if its performance at tasks T, as measured by P, improves with experience E.

---

[1]In his postdoc thesis, Fritzke (1998) termed the distance-based neural networks "vector-based", because they usually store knowledge in the form of vectors. I consider the term "distance-based" more precise, because it emphasizes the difference to the other class of pattern recognizers

Learning algorithms can be classified according to a number of criteria: supervised and unsupervised, statistical and instantaneous ("one-shot"), hard and soft, eager and lazy, neural and classical, batch and online...

Supervised learning covers classification and regression, where the correct output value is provided with each training datum. It is as if an imaginary supervisor or teacher provides the information to the pattern recognition system and guides it through the training. For unsupervised learning, there is no desired output and such algorithms are often called self-organizing. These algorithms include clustering, but are not limited to them. Between supervised and unsupervised, a third paradigm exists: reinforcement learning. Here, the supervisor checks the output which the pattern recognizer produces when presented training data and gives only a binary feedback: correct or wrong. This approach is much less efficient than supervised learning. The main challenge is the so-called credit assignment: From the right/wrong information alone it is, in general, hard to deduce which system parameters to adjust and how. In this thesis, only the first two categories are considered.

A general algorithm is considered to be "batch" if it first collects all data before processing them, while an "on-line" algorithm processes data one-by-one, as they become available. In many cases, a learning strategy can be implemented both in batch and on-line manner. On-line algorithms are applicable to very large training sets, or to a continuously incoming stream of sensor data. If the sampling can be considered random and the data contain redundancies, on-line algorithms can converge considerably faster than their batch counterparts. This is due to the fact that a random sample from a redundant set can contain almost as much information as the whole set. Batch algorithms have to spend the computing power also on the redundancies before approaching the solution, but are more stable.

The concepts of hard and soft learning are similar to the concepts of local and global knowledge representation. Concisely, local and global representation differ in the way how they cover the *input space*. Hard and soft learning differ in the way they cover the *parameter space*. In every step, hard learning identifies a small, fixed-sized subset of system parameters, sharing the same responsibility for a specific output, and modifies only them. In soft learning, a larger set of parameters, often of a variable size, is considered responsible for an answer, but the responsibility is usually weighted. The amount of adaptation depends on parameters' degree of responsibility for the answer. The difference can be well observed on the on-line versions of two unsupervised algorithms, K-means and SOM. In the first, only one of the means (prototypes) is adjusted in every step, whereas in SOM also the neighbors are modified, usually to a lesser degree.

1.3.3 Recall mechanism

Recall is normally applied to new, unseen, and thus unlabeled data. For many systems, the recall is straightforward once the system has been trained. In classification, one can differentiate between hard and soft recall. Hard recall gives an unambiguous answer to a new input and normally results in crisp, hard borders between classes. Soft recall produces fuzzy answers, like probabilities that the datum belongs to a class.

In case of the so-called "lazy learners" (which are actually nearest-neighbor classifiers and their variants), the recall behavior can be influenced even after training. This is because the decision how to generalize is deferred until a new datum is presented. In case of a K-nearest neighbors classifier, the choice of K influences the recall. The value of K is irrelevant for learning and can be changed at any moment during recall.

1.4 Outline of the thesis

This thesis is organized as follows: first, in Chapter 2 distance measures and averages for strings are discussed, as well as similarities. Novel distance measures and algorithms for finding averages are presented. They are constructed to fulfill the required mathematical properties and at the same time accommodate already existing knowledge about the string relationships, for example amino-acid mutabilities for applications in computational molecular biology. Practical problems concerning the computational complexity are also discussed. The functions from that chapter form the core of algorithms presented in Chapters 3 and 4. In Chapter 3, distance-based visualization and clustering algorithms are presented. It is shown how Sammon mapping – a classical visualization algorithm – can be applied to strings simply over a string metric. For clustering, string averages are used to adapt the well-known K-means algorithm for strings. Finally, as a combination of clustering and visualization, self-organizing maps for strings are presented.

Chapter 4 presents the classification methods relying on the distance measure and, possibly, average. As a representative for purely distance-based algorithm, the nearest-neighbor classifier is discussed. Due to its slow performance in recall, which is especially notable for strings, a new, improved version, called depleted nearest-neighbor is presented. As for algorithms based on data averages, the LVQ is presented and adapted for strings.

In Chapter 5 I turn to kernel-based methods. Based on the similarity and distance functions for strings, I define two kernels for strings and over them implement support vector machines for string classification. Finally, Chapter 6 discusses again clustering algorithms, this time in the light of graph theory and spectral analysis. These algorithms require only a general affinity function on the data and can thus be easily adapted to strings.

Each of the chapters first discusses the algorithms in their numeric version and then shows their application on string data. The algorithms are illustrated on example data sets, which are described at the end of this chapter. The last chapter gives a brief conclusion with an outlook on further developments.

Of the three branches of pattern recognition – clustering, classification and function approximation – only the first two are presented. I have not encountered a practical need for a mapping from strings onto a real-valued space. Should such a need emerge, many pattern classification algorithms can easily be adapted for the task of function approximation, for numerical data as well as for strings.

1.5 Data sets

For test purposes, several data sets were used. As easily comprehensible artificial data sets, a number of sets consistig of garbled English words were generated. Their purpose is mainly of illustrative nature. They were obtained by introducing noise – random replacements, insertions, and deletions of symbols – to seven English words: `railway`, `wolf`, `philosopher`, `underaged`, `distance`, `ice`, and `macrobiotics`. The alphabet consisted of the 26 lower-case Latin letters used in English. Sets with 40%, 50%, and even 75% noise were generated. The noise percentage is actually the probability for applying an edit operation at every position in the original string, but the care was taken that original words do not appear in them.

All replacement operations were equally likely, independent of the symbols involved. The same was true for insertions and deletions, but they appeared less often than replacements. The ratio was set to 2:1:1 for replacements, insertions and deletions, respectively. Example words are shown in Table 1.1.

For testing the data in the context of molecular biology, three different sets were used. One set of proteins, belonging to seven protein families, was chosen from the NCBI database (http://www.ncbi.nlm.nih.gov/entrez/query.fcgi). The choice of the families was made by a biologist. The families, described by their keywords, were: *protein tyrosine phosphatase, sodium channel, transducin, phospholipase C, phospholipase D, purinoceptor* and *cytochrome*. The set was obtained manually by taking a sample protein over the Entrez interface, performing a Blast search on the protein and choosing a number of high-scoring results.

Another biological set used in the experiments was the set of 320 hemoglobine α and β chain sequences, as used by Apostol and Szpankowski (1999). Hemoglobine is an approximately spherical protein (globin), responsible for oxygen transport into the tissue. It consists of two identical subunits (protomers), each made up of an α and a β chain. The chains have a similar structure, what makes them interesting for pattern recognition algorithms.

The third biological set comprised of 390 proteins from the kinase superfamily (Hanks and Quinn, 1991). The same data set was also used by Agrafiotis (1997). Kinases belong to the best-explored proteins and play an important role in many cellular activities. As enzymes, they are responsible for the transfer of phosphoryl groups from ATP (adenosine triphosphate) to other molecules and back. ATP is the most important energy carrier in cells and, by controlling the binding of the phosphoryl groups, kinases effectively regulate the energy flow in cells.

Using phylogenetic trees (Felsenstein, 1982), Hanks and Hunter (1995) have been able to recognize four main groups of kinases: ACG (71 samples in the set), CaMK (42 samples), CMGC (81) and PTK (104). Kinases not belonging to any of the four groups were labeled OPK (other protein kinases – 92 samples). To build the trees, they relied on a multiple sequence alignment (see 2), which they produced using "the old fashioned "eyeballing" technique", i.e. manually. In their words, "[w]hat is needed is an algorithm that first identifies and aligns the regions conserved throughout the entire family and leaves the more divergent regions, including the gap/insert segments, for last." Algorithms presented in this thesis are neither specifically tailored for such purpose, nor do they include the knowledge of an expert. Nevertheless, they produce results of the same quality, as I will show in the following chapters.

Phylogenetic trees allow for graphical representation of the sequence similarities under the assumption that the similarities are caused by evolution. They can be used as a basis for clustering the sequences, which can be performed manually by an expert, as in the above quoted work. If an automated clustering is desired, the sequence similarities suffice and the graphical representation is not needed. A number of clustering algorithms for this purpose is known, and a new, promising one is presented in Chapter 6.

Hanks and Quinn also anticipated the possibility of classifying unknown sequences using their similarity to the already known kinases, and proposed the use of the FASTA (Pearson and Lipman, 1988) database search program. It should be noted, however, that FASTA itself is not a classification program, but a tool for quickly finding similar sequences in a "database" (actually a large file). It can be applied in nearest-neighbor classifiers (Chapter 4), but, as I will show there, keeping all sequences in the database is not necessary. By reducing the number of sequences to compare, a significant speed-up in recall can be achieved.

Table 1.1: Sample garbled English words with 50% noise used in experiments. Even for an English speaking reader, it is not straightforward to deduce the original word in all cases.

ice	wolf	railway	distance
kck	wyoff	ilbrdy	distancfe
ee	worf	raxiarway	destnpte
ipe	olf	raiwah	duistancde
icfk	wof	rafilay	diaice
ic	dforf	cneplwfay	djtace
gpe	otolp	zaifla	istnance
ikce	womf	waizan	riaythnxe
icyde	olf	railwy	ditmnpce
iclt	wouoxf	tailwaby	uistanaco
iics	iolf	zazpiulwby	csdvnh

underaged	philosopher	macrobiotics
unezaaed	phinlvosoplher	abropbuotics
undieraged	zhgnsphen	cacrobiouics
undeiaddd	paiolsohher	daxcmopivlbtcs
uderabed	philsopher	macrobnotics
undeceksd	phqiloropaer	msczobiobics
unueraaed	phiosomgfyaher	marobrotiwr
usderaged	bpijqkosrphr	marrgbjzb
undlraged	himlojoqzhhr	macrobiwic
uepnderxgep	piwowyyqhenr	vanopipwtvcs
deraggce	nxiloszopker	paribotic

Chapter 2

Distance Functions for Strings

In this chapter, properties of distance measures in general and distance measures for strings are discussed. The distance measure is the key element in distance-based algorithms. Distance is often defined on vector spaces, but is not limited to them. Having an arbitrary set $\mathcal{D}$, a function $d : \mathcal{D} \times \mathcal{D} \to \mathbf{R}$ is a distance measure, if for all $a, b, c \in \mathcal{D}$ the following is satisfied:

1. $d(a, b) \geq 0$,
2. $d(a, b) = 0 \Leftrightarrow a = b$,
3. $d(a, b) = d(b, a)$,
4. $d(a, b) + d(b, c) \geq d(a, c)$. \hfill (2.1)

It should be noted that the conditions are not independent: The first condition, positive semi-definiteness, follows automatically from the other three. For comprehensibility it is nevertheless customary to present them in this form, both in textbooks and in the scientific literature.

If each datum consists of purely real numerical values, like measurements of physical quantities, it is common to arrange them in a vector. Having no a priori indications against it, the Euclidean distance is the usual choice:

$$d(\boldsymbol{x}, \boldsymbol{y}) = \sqrt{\sum_i \| x[i] - y[i] \|^2}.$$

In special cases, another distance measure can be used. If, for example, the vector components are limited to the set $\{0, 1\}$, the vector can be regarded as a fixed-length binary string. In that case it is common to use the Hamming distance, which is the number of bits in which two strings differ:

$$d(\boldsymbol{x}, \boldsymbol{y}) = \sum_i (x[i] \otimes y[i]),$$

$\otimes$ denoting the "exclusive or" logical operation. Hamming distance is actually a special case of l_1 distance, also known as city-block distance or Manhattan distance, which is simply the sum of distances along each coordinate:

$$d(\boldsymbol{x}, \boldsymbol{y}) = \sum_i |x[i] - y[i]|.$$

Generalizing this idea, the Minkowski distance is obtained:

$$d(\boldsymbol{x}, \boldsymbol{y}) = \left(\sum_i |x[i] - y[i]|^\lambda \right)^{\frac{1}{\lambda}}.$$

Different distance measures highlight different data properties and can easily result in very different clustering and classification. Another factor greatly influencing results is scaling. This is especially true if the measuring units of vector components differ: how does one balance the influence of length and mass on a distance measure? Which are the appropriate units: meters, inches, or parsecs; electron-volts, kilograms or Sun masses? A usual solution is scaling to standard deviation along axes, but it bears some risks. If data are more stretched along one axis than another, this might be due to improper scaling, but also to cluster or class distribution along an axis. Scaling it down would hide the information. There is no general recipe for choosing either the suitable metric or the right scaling, and the decision has to be made in light of data and processing aims.

The same questions apply to symbol strings. Although strings are very different from vectors, various distance measures can be defined for them, too. This chapter presents a number of them, and also similarity functions, which are more common in computational molecular biology. As it will be shown, string distance is easily defined, but computing it is usually much more costly than for vectorial data. Based on distance, averages of strings are presented. Here, too, computing them is much more expensive than computing the mean of vectorial data. Moreover, as it will be shown, the computational costs are generally so huge that, as a rule, we can only hope to find an approximate solution.

Strings are very common objects in everyday life. For example, this thesis consists mostly of strings. To apply pattern recognition methods on strings, the functions used by the methods have to be defined on them. Nearest neighbor classifiers require only a distance function to be defined and are easily adapted for strings. To apply methods like K-means and LVQ, one also needs to compute some kind of average of strings. Support vector machines take a different approach and rely only on a kernel function. This chapter discusses similarity and distance functions for strings. Kernel functions based on similarity are discussed in Chapter 5.

2.1 Basic distance functions for strings

A *string* s is a one-dimensional data structure, a succession of *symbols* or *characters* from some alphabet. By one-dimensional we mean that the position of each symbol in the string is determined by one parameter, its *index* i in the string. The index is always a positive integer[1]. The length of the string is denoted by $|s|$, and the symbol at the position i by $s[i]$. The zero-length *empty string* is also allowed. It contains no symbols and is usually denoted by ε. A *substring* $s[i \ldots j]$ is the string consisting of symbols $s[i], s[i + 1], \ldots, s[j]$ at positions $1, 2, \ldots, j - i + 1$, respectively. Special cases are the *prefix* $s[1 \ldots i]$, which is the substring consisting of the first i symbols of s, and *suffix* $s[i \ldots |s|]$, consisting of all symbols of s starting from the index i.

If two strings have the same length, the simplest distance measure is the above mentioned Hamming distance, that is, the number of positions at which the symbols in the strings differ. For example, the Hamming distance between the strings sidestep and sideline is four, for they differ in the last four symbols. However, even for equal-length strings the Hamming distance easily leads to "unnatural" results. Consider the strings looking and outlook. Intuitively, we would consider the two strings somewhat similar, at least more similar than any of them is to the string sparked. But, writing them one above the other:

```
looking
outlook
```

we note that they differ at all seven positions. For strings of different lengths Hamming distance is not applicable at all.

A simple and computationally very effective "distance" measure for general strings is the feature distance (Kohonen, 1985). In this context, a feature is a short substring, typically 2 or 3 symbols long, usually referred to as N-gram, N being the length of the substring. To compute feature distance between two strings, one collects all such substrings of each string. Because information about the order of the features is not retained, the strings are usually extended by special markers at the beginning and the end, and these markers are also included as symbols when constructing features. The feature distance is then, simply put, the number of features two strings differ in. More precisely, having two strings s and t and their corresponding collections of features $\mathcal{F}_s$ and $\mathcal{F}_t$ (which are, strictly speaking, not sets, because they can have repeating elements), the feature distance is defined as:

$$d(s, t) := \max(|\mathcal{F}_s|, |\mathcal{F}_t|) - |\mathcal{F}_s \cap \mathcal{F}_t| \qquad (2.2)$$

---

[1]For technical reasons, some notations allow the index to be a non-negative integer, i.e. the first symbol in the string has the index 0, the second 1 and so on.

where $|\mathcal{F}_s \cap \mathcal{F}_s|$ denotes the number of common features in both strings. The method is very popular for its speed and simplicity and has been successfully used in speech recognition (Kohonen, 1985). However, it must be noted that this measure is not a distance, for two different strings can have zero distance, which contradicts the requirement (2) in Equation (2.1).

To see this, consider two strings, s = AABA and t = ABAA. Using $\triangleright$ and $\triangleleft$ to mark the beginning and the end of each string respectively and using substrings of length two (bigrams) as features, the corresponding feature collections are:

$$\mathcal{F}_s = \{\triangleright A, AA, AB, BA, A\triangleleft\} \quad \text{and} \quad \mathcal{F}_t = \{\triangleright A, AB, BA, AA, A\triangleleft\}$$

As mentioned previously, the order of features is not retained in their collections, therefore the two feature collections above are equal and the feature distance is consequently zero.

It may be noted that FASTA (Pearson and Lipman, 1988), a popular database searching algorithm used in molecular biology, pursues a similar strategy in its first step for finding good candidates. In the terminology of molecular biology, a database is simply a file containing a possibly huge number of amino-acid or DNA sequences, usually annotated with additional information. Sequences there are simply long strings, every symbol standing for an amino-acid or nucleotide base. FASTA is applied for finding sequences in the database which are similar to the user-provided search sequence. Contrary to the above method, FASTA does not ignore the positions of the matching substrings.

Another very common distance measure for strings is the Levenshtein distance (Levenshtein, 1966), also known as the edit distance. It measures the minimum effort needed to transform one string into another. A string is transformed into another by applying basic edit operations: replacement, insertion and deletion of a symbol. Insertion and deletion are inverse processes, and are often referred together as *indel*. Each of the three operations has a cost assigned to it. This set of operations is redundant: a replacement can be performed by a successive insertion and deletion of symbols, but it is convenient to have it as a distinct operation. In most real-world applications, insertion, deletion and replacement of a symbol are physically distinct processes, with different likelihood of appearance. Allowing only insertion and deletion as edit operations would imply the cost of a replacement to be the sum of the costs for the insertion and the deletion, which does not generally reflect the reality. On the contrary, in many cases a replacement is more likely to occur than an insertion or a deletion, and is consequently less costly than each of them. In other words, less effort is generally needed to repair a distorted symbol than to reconstruct a missing one. The same holds for insertions, because distance is a symmetrical function: the cost of deleting a symbol in one string to obtain the other must be the same as inserting the missing symbol in the second string to obtain the first one. This will be discussed below, in context of the weighted Levenshtein distance (WLD). For now, let us suppose that all edit operations are equally likely.

The sequence of edit operations applied to transform one string into another can be coded itself in a string, called *edit transcript*. Symbols appearing in it are R (replace), I (insert), D (delete), and M (match), meaning no edit operation is needed. For example, take the strings motivation and intentional. The transcript for transforming the former into latter is RRMRRDMMMMII. This can be graphically represented by writing and aligning the strings above each other:

```
motivation
RRMRRDMMMMII
inten tional
```

Assuming the same cost for all edit operations, the edit distance is simply the number of symbols in the transcript that are not "M". In the above case, the distance between the strings is seven.

It should be obvious that a string can be transformed into another in an infinite number of ways, and that many of them will carry different costs with them. Therefore, the Levenshtein distance is defined as the cost of the cheapest transformation. Sometimes the cheapest transformation is ambiguous, because there is more than one transformation with the same minimal cost. This does not pose a problem, since the distance is concerned only with the cost itself, and not with the path that led to it. However, as we shall see later, the path might be interesting when computing the average over a set of strings.

Finding the minimal cost is commonly done by dynamic programming. The original algorithm was probably discovered and rediscovered independently many times in different contexts (Sankoff and Kruskal, 1983, Setubal and Meidanis, 1997), e.g. by Wagner and Fischer (1974) for automatic spelling correction and finding the longest common subsequence. In molecular biology, the credit is given to Needleman and Wunsch (1970). The algorithm is extensively discussed e.g. in (Gusfield, 1997). Here, only a brief overview describing the concept is given.

Basically, the idea is to start with empty prefixes of the strings s_1 and s_2 for which the distance is sought. The distance between such prefixes is zero. Then, one of the prefixes is extended by one character and the distance to the other prefix computed. Note that the distance between any string and the empty string is equal to the string length: $d(s, \varepsilon) = |s|$. Therefore, the distance between such an extended prefix and the zero-length prefix of the other string is straightforward to compute. The prefix is further extended and the distance computed until the whole string is covered and the distance between its every prefix and the empty string is establlshed. The same is done with the other string, taking the zero-length prefix of the first string. Both results are most conveniently written orthognnal to

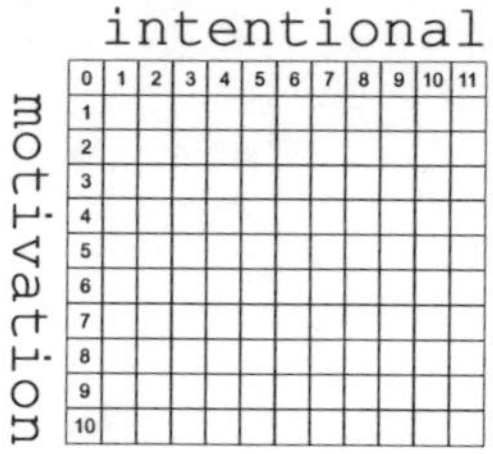

intentional

	0	1	2	3	4	5	6	7	8	9	10	11
0												
1												
2												
3												
4												
5												
6												
7												
8												
9												
10												

(left edge: motivation)

intentional

	0	1	2	3	4	5	6	7	8	9	10	11
0	0	1	2	3	4	5	6	7	8	9	10	11
1	1	1	2	3	4	5	6	7	8	9	10	11
2	2	2	2	3	4	5	6	7	7	8	9	10
3	3	3	3	2								
4												
5												
6												
7												
8												
9												
10												

(left edge: motivation)

Figure 2.1: Table used for computing string distances. One string is written along the left edge of the table and the other along its top edge. The top row and the leftmost column contain the distances between the empty string and all prefixes of the adjacent string.

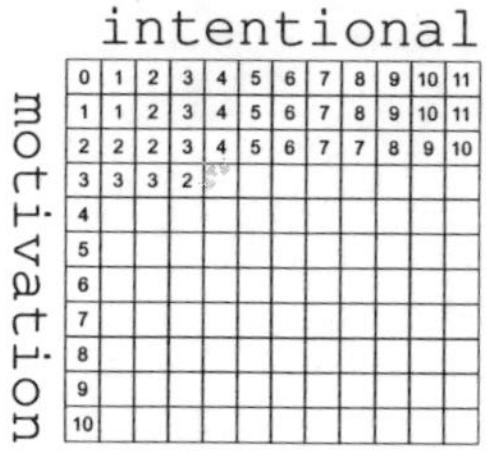

Figure 2.2: Filling up the table. After the first row and column have been computed, every cell in the table can be computed from the three previously computed cells, taking into account if the symbols in the strings match at the position defined by cell position in the table.

each other at the edges of a table (Figure 2.1). The top row contains the distances between the empty string and the prefixes of s_2 (intentional in this example), whereas the left column contains the distances between the empty string and the prefixes of s_1 (motivation). The intent is to have a table where the entry (i, j) is the distance between the $s_1[1 \ldots i]$ and the prefix $s_2[1 \ldots j]$. Let us denote this entry by $D(i, j)$. To allow empty prefixes, the table includes a 0-th row (top) and a 0-th column (left), computed as described.

In order to compute the remaining cells, we proceed recursively. Assuming that the distances $D(i-1, j-1)$, $D(i-1, j)$, and $D(i, j-1)$ for the corresponding prefixes have already been computed, there are only three possibilities for the distance $D(i, j)$:

1. Starting from the prefixes $s_1[1 \ldots i-1]$ and $s_2[1 \ldots j-1]$, both are extended by one symbol. If both symbols match, the distance remains unchanged. Otherwise, the distance is increased by one:

$$D(i, j) = D(i - 1, j - 1) + \text{mismatch}(s_1[i], s_2[j])$$

The function "mismatch" above is defined to return 0 if two symbols are equal and 1 otherwise.

2. Starting from the prefixes $s_1[1 \ldots i - 1]$ and $s_2[1 \ldots j]$, the former is extended by one symbol whereas the latter is kept fixed. Thus the additional symbol $s_1[i]$ cannot be matched with a symbol in $s_2[1 \ldots j]$. To obtain a

intentional

		i	n	t	e	n	t	i	o	n	a	l
	0	1	2	3	4	5	6	7	8	9	10	11
m	1	1	2	3	4	5	6	7	8	9	10	11
o	2	2	2	3	4	5	6	7	7	8	9	10
t	3	3	3	2	3	4	5	6	7	8	9	10
i	4	3	4	3	3	4	5	5	6	7	8	9
v	5	4	4	4	4	4	5	6	6	7	8	9
a	6	5	5	5	5	5	5	6	7	7	7	8
t	7	6	6	5	6	6	5	6	7	8	8	8
i	8	7	7	6	6	7	6	5	6	7	8	9
o	9	8	8	7	7	7	7	6	5	6	7	8
n	10	9	8	8	8	7	8	7	6	5	6	7

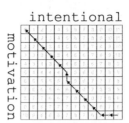

intentional

Figure 2.3: The full table contains in each cell the distance between corresponding prefixes of the strings. Particularly, the last, bottom-right cell contains the distance between the complete strings.

Figure 2.4: Backtracking through the table. Based on the values in each cell, one can reconstruct which edit operation – reflected by a horizontal, vertical or diagonal step – was optimal at each position. All steps together form the optimal path.

match, $s_1[i]$ would have to be inserted after the position j in s_2, or deleted from s_1. Either way, this increases the distance by one:

$$D(i, j) = D(i - 1, j) + 1$$

3. Starting from the prefixes $s_1[1 \ldots i]$ and $s_2[1 \ldots j-1]$, the latter is extended by one symbol whereas the former is kept fixed. Thus the additional symbol $s_2[j]$ cannot be matched with a symbol in $s_1[1 \ldots i]$. To obtain a match, $s_2[j]$ would have to be inserted after the position i in s_1, or deleted from s_2. Either way, this increases the distance by one:

$$D(i, j) = D(i, j - 1) + 1$$

The distance is defined as the *minimal* transformation cost, so over the three possibilities, the distance $D(i, j)$ is defined as:

$$D(i, j) = \min (\ D(i - 1, j - 1) + \text{mismatch}(s_1[i], s_2[j]),$$
$$D(i - 1, j) + 1,$$
$$D(i, j - 1) + 1\ ) \tag{2.3}$$

Using Equation (2.3), the table is filled up, e.g. row-wise, like in Figure 2.2. In the complete table (Figure 2.3), the last, bottom right cell contains the Levenshtein distance between the strings. For many applications, not only the distance, but also the edit transcript is required. It can be reconstructed from the table and the strings. We start from the last cell and examine its three neighboring cells: – left, left-above, and above – to see from which we one arrived to it. In other words, we examine which of the three terms in Equation (2.3) was minimal. This leads us to the next cell, which is examined in the same way an so on, until we reach the table beginning, the top left cell. The path through the table (Figure 2.4), encodes the edit transcript: horizontal steps stand for "insert", vertical for "delete", and diagonal for "match" or "replace", depending on the symbols at the corresponding positions. The alignment of the strings is easily produced from the edit transcript: at "match" and "replace" positions, the symbols from the strings are aligned with each other. At "delete" positions, the symbol from the first string is aligned with a space between two symbols in the second string. The opposite is true for "insert": symbols from the second string are aligned with spaces in the first. The choice, which string is the first and which the second makes no difference for distance and alignment. Only in the edit transcript "I"s and "D" are swapped.

It should be noted that the path through the table, the edit transcript, and the alignment are not unique. For the same two strings, an equally valid result is:

```
motivation
RRMDRRMMMMII
int entional
```

also having the edit distance of seven. There is no optimal solution to this ambiguity. In practice, alignment algorithms are usually constructed to prefer one path direction, e.g. diagonal, over the other two.

In the above example, we considered only the case when all basic edit operations have the same cost. But when they do not, the distance function is usually referred to as weighted edit (Levenshtein) distance. This includes very common cases, where replacements of different symbols appear with different probabilities and are therefore assigned different costs, specific for each symbol-to-symbol transformation, as well as the above mentioned case, where insertions and deletions are more expensive than replacements. The weighted distance can be computed in much the same, recursive fashion as the simple:

$$D(i,j) = \min(\ D(i-1,j-1) + \text{cost}(s_1[i], s_2[j]),$$
$$D(i-1,j) + w_d, \qquad\qquad (2.4)$$
$$D(i,j-1) + w_i \ )$$

The function "cost" returns the cost of replacing $s_1[i]$ with $s_2[j]$, w_d is the cost of deleting the symbol $s_1[i]$ and w_i the cost of inserting $s_2[j]$. Depending on the chosen costs, the "weighted edit distance" can cease to be a distance in the strict mathematical sense. For example, if $w_i \neq w_d$, the symmetry relation is not satisfied.

Edit distances can be applied everywhere where transmissions of string signals over noisy channels are involved. Telecommunication is one such example, evolution another one.

2.2 Similarity functions for strings

Especially in molecular biology, another measure, the *similarity* is often used to describe the relationship between two strings. Similarity is simpler than distance. Any function $s : S^2 \to \mathbb{R}$ can be declared a similarity function – the question is only if it reflects the natural relationship between the data. In practice, such functions are often symmetrical and assign a higher value to two identical elements than to distinct ones, but this is not required.

For strings, similarity is closely related to alignment. Alignments were implicitly used above when discussing edit transcripts. For completeness, I quote here a textbook definition of alignment:

> A (global) alignment of two strings S1 and S2 is obtained by first inserting chosen spaces (or dashes), either into or at the ends of S1 and S2, and then placing the two resulting strings one above the other so that every character or space in either string is opposite a unique character or a unique space in the other string.
> (Gusfield, 1997)

The spaces (or dashes) are special symbols, not from the alphabet over which the strings are defined. They are used to mark positions in a string where the symbol from the other string is not aligned with any symbol. For the above example with the strings motivation and intentional,

```
motiv-ation--
int-en-tional
```

is an alignment, not necessarily optimal. Each alignment can be assigned a score according to certain rules. In most simple cases, a similarity score is assigned to each pair of symbols in the alphabet, as well as to pairs of a symbol and a space. The score for two aligned strings is computed as the sum of similarity scores of their aligned symbols and the similarity of the strings is defined as the score of their highest-scoring alignment. Such an alignment can be found by dynamic programming, in much the same way as the edit distance. Only this time, for computing each cell in the table, not the minimum over the three distances from previous cells is sought, but the maximum over the three similarities.

In computational molecular biology, similarity is most often computed for DNA or amino-acid sequences (sequence and string are used as synonyms here), where similarity between symbols is established empirically to reflect observed mutability/stability of symbols. For DNA sequences, the alphabet consists of only four symbols: A, T, G, and C, standing for the four nucleotide bases which build the DNA. In case of amino-acid sequences, there are 20 different symbols, one for every amino-acid appearing in nature. Due to mutations, different amino acids can be more or less easily substituted with others, and depending on their biochemical properties, such mutations may be more or less likely to be accepted by evolution. In other words, some mutations lead to extinction of a species, so the similarity between involved amino-acids can be regarded as low. Other mutations might have no obvious influence on the survivability of the species and the involved amino-acids can be considered similar.

Because each pair of symbols can have a different similarity and no obvious regularity exists, similarities are usually stored in look-up tables, which have the form of a quadratic matrix. Among scoring matrices, the PAM (point accepted mutations) (Dayhoff et al., 1978) and BLOSUM (block substitution matrix) (Henikoff and Henikoff, 1992) families are the most often used. For covering all possible symbol combinations, the matrices need 20 rows and 20 columns. The 21st row and column are needed for the similarity between a symbol and space. In practice, three more rows and columns are often used, for three special symbols occasionally used in amino-acid sequences: **B**, standing for aspartate *or* asparagine, **Z** for glutamate *or* glutamine, and **X** for any amino-acid.

2.3   Similarity and distance

Many pattern recognition methods, which will be presented in chapters 3 and 4, are defined over a distance measure, not similarity. Intuitively, it is clear that these two measures are somehow related: the higher the similarity between strings, the lower the distance between them should be. But, in contrast to a similarity score, which can be defined in a fairly arbitrary (although not always meaningful) manner, a distance must satisfy the four requirements (2.1). For strings one can use the Levenshtein distance, weighted in some way. Although it can be computed directly, in cases where there are already devised scoring schemes – like in computational molecular biology – it is desirable to compute a distance that is consistent with the similarity score of the strings. By consistent distance I mean a function, which assigns a lower distance value to strings with higher similarity score. This can be achieved by appropriate weighting of edit operation costs.

A simple method for computing "distance" from similarity score for proteins was applied by Agrafiotis (1997). For computing the score he used normalized scoring matrices with values scaled to $[0, 1]$, and for spaces he used a fixed value of 0.1. Then he computed the scores for all pairs of proteins from his data set and ordered them into a new matrix S. The element $S[i][j]$ of this similarity matrix was the similarity score for the i-th and j-th protein from the data set. This matrix was subsequently also scaled to $[0, 1]$. The distance between i-th and j-th protein was then computed as

$$D[i][j] = 1 - S[i][j].$$

This approach has several disadvantages: First, the computational and storage overheads are obvious. In most applications pairwise similarity scores of all data are not needed. Also, this method is not applicable for on-line algorithms, with data sets of unknown and maybe even infinite sizes. But more than that, it is not clear, if the above function is a distance at all. Although Agrafiotis did not elaborate on that, it is easy to see that simple scaling of the S matrix can lead to a situation where the requirement (2) for distance is violated. Such a case appears when the diagonal elements – standing for self-similarities of strings – are not all equal. A workaround, like attempt to scale the matrix row- or column-wise, so that the diagonal elements are all ones, would cause a violation of the symmetry relationship (3). Element $S[i][j]$ would generally be scaled differently than $S[j][i]$ so the two would not be equal any more. And finally, the triangle inequality – requirement (4) – is not guaranteed to be satisfied.

Setubal and Meidanis (1997, pp. 92-96) propose a more mathematically founded method for computing distance from similarity score and vice versa. Starting from an arbitrary constant M, they define

$$p(\alpha, \beta) \quad = \quad M - c(\alpha, \beta) \quad \text{and} \tag{2.5}$$

$$g \quad = \quad \frac{M}{2} - h. \tag{2.6}$$

where $p(\alpha, \beta)$ is the similarity score for the symbols α and β, $c(\alpha, \beta)$ is the cost of replacing α with β, g is the value of space in the alignment (usually a negative one) and h is the cost of an insertion or a deletion. The function $c(\alpha, \beta)$ is defined to be non-negative, symmetric and greater than zero for $\alpha \neq \beta$, and $h > 0$. The distance between the two strings s_1 and s_2, $d(s_1, s_2)$ is then the minimum sum of individual costs of operations needed for transforming one string into the other. The distance $d(s_1, s_2)$ and the similarity score, which will here be denoted as $\langle s_1 | s_2 \rangle$, are related by the formula:

$$\langle s_1 | s_2 \rangle + d(s_1, s_2) = \frac{M}{2} \cdot (|s_1| + |s_2|). \tag{2.7}$$

Computing the distance is then done by first computing the similarity score according to a suitable scoring scheme and subsequently applying the above formula.

Although simple and straightforward, the above method implies a requirement on the cost function $c(\alpha, \beta)$ which is seldom met in practice. From the above it follows that

$$c(\alpha, \alpha) = M - p(\alpha, \alpha).$$

However, the requirement (2) for distance functions implies that $c(\alpha, \alpha) = 0$ for every α. Since M is a constant, it follows that $p(\alpha, \alpha)$ must be equal to M for every α, or otherwise the function $d(s_1, s_2)$ would not be a distance. Unfortunately, this condition is not satisfied for scoring matrices used in computational molecular biology, like PAM or BLOSUM, where diagonal elements – determining the similarity of amino acids with themselves – have different values. Consequently, the above method cannot be used in comparing amino acid sequences.

Therefore I propose another method for computing distance from similarity score (Fischer, 2002). Recall that distance in a vector space can be computed over a norm, which, in turn, is computed over an inner product:

$$
\begin{aligned}
d(\boldsymbol{x}, \boldsymbol{y}) &= \|\boldsymbol{x} - \boldsymbol{y}\| \\
&= \sqrt{\langle \boldsymbol{x} - \boldsymbol{y}, \boldsymbol{x} - \boldsymbol{y} \rangle} \\
&= \sqrt{\langle \boldsymbol{x}, \boldsymbol{x} \rangle + \langle \boldsymbol{y}, \boldsymbol{y} \rangle - 2\langle \boldsymbol{x}, \boldsymbol{y} \rangle}.
\end{aligned}
$$

We shall use this as a motivation and, by analogy, define the distance for strings over their similarity score:

$$
d(\boldsymbol{s}_1, \boldsymbol{s}_2) = \left(\langle \boldsymbol{s}_1 | \boldsymbol{s}_1 \rangle + \langle \boldsymbol{s}_2 | \boldsymbol{s}_2 \rangle - 2\langle \boldsymbol{s}_1 | \boldsymbol{s}_2 \rangle \right)^{1/n}. \tag{2.8}
$$

The perfect analogy is achieved for $n = 2$. Although this analogy might seem far-fetched, we shall see that this function satisfies all the properties of the distance if the similarity scheme obeys some simple rules. Depending on the scoring scheme, the function might be a distance function even for different n. It will be shown below that a distance function can be defined using the BLOSUM62 scoring scheme and $n = 1$. In general, we require, that the similarity of a symbol with itself is always positive:

$$
p(\alpha, \alpha) > 0. \tag{2.9}
$$

Second, we require that every symbol is at least as similar to itself as to any other symbol:

$$
\begin{aligned}
p(\alpha, \beta) &\leq p(\alpha, \alpha) \\
p(\alpha, \beta) &\leq p(\beta, \beta)
\end{aligned} \quad \text{for all } \alpha, \beta \in \Sigma. \tag{2.10}
$$

The similarity function is, as always, symmetrical:

$$
p(\alpha, \beta) = p(\beta, \alpha). \tag{2.11}
$$

Spaces in aligned strings can be considered symbols with a fixed small similarity value for all non-spaces:

$$
p(-, \alpha) = g \leq p(\alpha, \beta) \quad \text{for all } \alpha, \beta \neq -. \tag{2.12}
$$

Spaces should never be aligned with spaces, but it is convenient to define a score also for that case, because then we can consider strings $\boldsymbol{s}_1$ and $\boldsymbol{s}_2$ to be aligned (i.e. to allow spaces in them) and nevertheless compute the correct similarity score of a string with itself. When the aligned string contains spaces, computing its similarity with itself leads to a computation of similarity of two spaces. Defining

$$p(-,-) = 0$$

ensures that the self-similarity score of an aligned string (a string that may contain spaces) is the same as of its non-aligned (space-free) variant.

We consider optimally aligned strings, which, by definition, have the same length. Their similarity score is then equal to the sum of the individual similarity scores of their aligned symbols:

$$\langle s_1 | s_2 \rangle = \sum_i p(\alpha_i, \beta_i). \tag{2.13}$$

Then, the requirements (1) – (3) for a distance are easy to prove. It is obvious that the distance is symmetric, because the similarity function is symmetric. Relying on (2.10) we get:

$$\begin{aligned}
\langle s_1 | s_1 \rangle + \langle s_2 | s_2 \rangle - 2\langle s_1 | s_2 \rangle \;\; &\geq \;\; \langle s_1 | s_1 \rangle + \langle s_2 | s_2 \rangle - \langle s_1 | s_1 \rangle - \langle s_1 | s_2 \rangle \\
&\geq \;\; \langle s_1 | s_1 \rangle + \langle s_2 | s_2 \rangle - \langle s_1 | s_1 \rangle - \langle s_2 | s_2 \rangle \\
&= \;\; 0. \tag{2.14}
\end{aligned}$$

That is, the distance measure is also positive semi-definite. Also, when the distance is equal to zero:

$$\langle s_1 | s_1 \rangle + \langle s_1 | s_1 \rangle - 2\langle s_1 | s_1 \rangle = 0 \tag{2.15}$$

it can be written as

$$\langle s_1 | s_1 \rangle + \langle s_2 | s_2 \rangle = \langle s_1 | s_2 \rangle + \langle s_1 | s_2 \rangle. \tag{2.16}$$

Recalling again that two symbols have the highest similarity when they are identical (2.10), it follows:

$$\begin{aligned}
\langle s_1 | s_1 \rangle \;\; &= \;\; \langle s_1 | s_2 \rangle \quad \text{and} \\
\langle s_2 | s_2 \rangle \;\; &= \;\; \langle s_1 | s_2 \rangle \tag{2.17}
\end{aligned}$$

meaning that $s_1 = s_2$.

Finally, the triangle inequality condition (4) is satisfied if the similarity obeys one more rule. Let us start with $n = 1$. The condition is:

$$\begin{aligned}
d(s_1, s_2) + d(s_2, s_3) \;\; &\geq \;\; d(s_1, s_3), \text{ that is,} \\
\langle s_1 | s_1 \rangle + \langle s_2 | s_2 \rangle - 2\langle s_1 | s_2 \rangle \;\; + \;\; \langle s_2 | s_2 \rangle + \langle s_3 | s_3 \rangle - 2\langle s_2 | s_3 \rangle & \\
\geq \;\; \langle s_1 | s_1 \rangle + \langle s_3 | s_3 \rangle - 2\langle s_1 | s_3 \rangle. \tag{2.18}
\end{aligned}$$

Adding $\langle s_1|s_1\rangle$ and subtracting $\langle s_3|s_3\rangle$ on both sides, reordering and dividing the inequality by two we get:

$$\langle s_1|s_1\rangle - \langle s_1|s_2\rangle + \langle s_2|s_2\rangle - \langle s_2|s_3\rangle \geq \langle s_1|s_1\rangle - \langle s_1|s_3\rangle \qquad (2.19)$$

which means nothing more than that the sum of drops in similarity (i.e. the price we pay in terms of similarity score) when replacing s_1 with s_2, and then replacing s_2 with s_3 must be at least equal to the price for replacing s_1 directly with s_3. This is a plausible condition, which is satisfied in BLOSUM62, currently probably the most popular scoring matrix for proteins. We can call the condition above strong triangle inequality for similarity. It can be made weaker by using $n > 1$. For example, for $n = 2$, after squaring the inequality, we get:

$$\langle s_1|s_1\rangle + \langle s_2|s_2\rangle - 2\langle s_1|s_2\rangle \;+\; \langle s_2|s_2\rangle + \langle s_3|s_3\rangle - 2\langle s_2|s_3\rangle +$$
$$+2\, d(s_1,s_2)\, d(s_2,s_3) \;\geq\; \langle s_1|s_1\rangle + \langle s_3|s_3\rangle - 2\langle s_1|s_3\rangle. \qquad (2.20)$$

Adding $\langle s_1|s_1\rangle - \langle s_3|s_3\rangle$ left and right, and dividing the result by two, we obtain:

$$\langle s_1|s_1\rangle - \langle s_1|s_2\rangle + \langle s_2|s_2\rangle - \langle s_2|s_3\rangle \;+$$
$$+\, d(s_1,s_2)d(s_2,s_3) \;\geq\; \langle s_1|s_1\rangle - \langle s_1|s_3\rangle. \qquad (2.21)$$

Since $d(s_1, s_2)$ and $d(s_2, s_3)$ are always positive by definition, this inequality is easier to satisfy than the strong triangle inequality. PAM40, PAM120 and PAM250 scoring matrices satisfy this inequality already for $n = 2$.

Note: One might be tempted to see distance as the exact opposite to similarity. This is not the case: as in vector spaces a larger scalar product does not always imply a smaller distance between vectors (this is true only for vectors of the same lengths), larger similarity does not necessarily lead to smaller distance between sequences, both in this as in the Setubal-Meidanis approach. The reason is that similarity depends strongly on string lengths, whereas distance generally does not.

Example: Let us take $M = 2$, $\mathrm{cost}(\alpha, \beta) = 0$ for $\alpha = \beta$ and $\mathrm{cost}(\alpha, \beta) = 1$ for $\alpha \neq \beta$, and $h = 1$ (unweighted Levenshtein distance). The corresponding scoring scheme is $p(\alpha, \beta) = 2$ for identical and 1 for different symbols, and $g = 0$. Now consider the string AX, compared to AB and to AXCD. In the first case, the two As match, but X and B do not, leading to the similarity score equal to 3 and a distance of 1. In the second case, the first two symbols in both strings match, leading to the similarity score of four and the distance of two. Both the similarity and the distance are higher than in the first case.

2.4   Implementation issues

The dimensions of the dynamic programming table used for computing distance and similarity rise with string lengths. The number of rows in the table is one

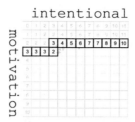

Figure 2.5: Saving space in dynamic programming. To compute the rest of the row, only the highlighted cells in the table are required. The remaining cells need not be stored.

more than the length of the first string, and the number of columns one more than the length of the second one. If the strings have approximately the same length, the number of cells rises with the square of the length. For very long strings, like those commonly appearing in molecular biology, this can pose serious problems: Both the time needed for computing the table, as well as the memory required for storing it, rise proportionally with the number of cells. The problem of memory has been more acute, but fortunately also easier to solve by a divide-and-conquer strategy (Hirshberg, 1975). The computing time can also be reduced under certain circumstances, although generally not as much as the memory requirements.

2.4.1 Reducing memory requirements

We have seen that in the fully computed table the last cell contains the distance between the strings, or similarity, if we applied the corresponding algorithm. Also, every cell in the table contains the distance (similarity) of the corresponding string prefixes. Recall that for computing each cell, we needed only three adjacent cells: left, above, and left-above of the current one. The result has to be stored only until all further cells adjacent to it are computed, and can be discarded afterwards. There are three such cells: the one right to the current one, the one below it and the one right-below. That means that if we fill the table row-wise, we need only to keep the cells above and to the left of the not yet computed ones in memory (Figure 2.5). The cells in the 0-th row and column depend only on the corresponding position in the string and on no other cells, and can be computed on-the-fly, when needed.

This method reduces the memory requirements significantly: instead of quadratic, the space complexity is now linear. However, in order to compute the alignment of the strings (or edit transcript), we have backtracked through the table. Finding the alignment can be done without storing the whole table, but with a little more computation. The divide-and-conquer approach is to divide the problem recursively into two smaller ones, until the solution is obvious.

It is obvious that the same alignment can be computed backwards, by start-ing from the end of the strings and propagating towards their beginning. In other words, the table can be equally well filled from the bottom right corner left- and upwards. This is identical to reversing the strings, computing the table in the or-dinary fashion, and then mirroring it along the main anti-diagonal. In the ordinary table, the values in the cells – the distances of the string prefixes tend to rise as we progress towards the bottom right corner of the table. In the table computed backwards, the distances rise in the opposite direction, towards the top-left corner. With a little caution, due to the extra 0-th row and column, we can add the two tables. It is straightforward to show that in the sum, the cells on the optimal path (describing the optimal string alignment) have the same value, which is the lowest in the table. (If we would work with similarities instead of distances, the optimal path cells would have the highest score). For computing the alignment, it thus suffices to locate these cells.

The basic idea how to do this without keeping the whole table in memory is the following: the technique depicted in (Figure 2.5) produces ultimately the last row in the table. When computing the table backwards, the result is the first (top) row of the table. In the divide-and-conquer approach, the idea is to split one string into two halves: a prefix and a suffix. The distance between the other string and the *prefix* is computed in the forward manner, resulting in a row in the middle of the distance table. Propagating backwards, the distance between the *suffix* and the other string is computed. This again produces the middle row, but now of the backward table. Adding the two rows together, a row in the sum table is obtained. The cell with the lowest distance in it is a cell on the optimal path and its position has to be stored. To find other cells on the path, we proceed recursively: we split the prefix and the suffix further in halves and repeat the process for each until the splitting produces empty substrings. Having all the cells on the path, the alignment and edit transcript are straightforward to deduce.

This might seem a computationally expensive approach, since we compute the same cells it the table over and over again, only to retain the currently interesting one. This is only partially true. Recall that the optimal path always goes from top left towards bottom right in the table. It can never go up or left, because positions in the strings are only allowed to increase in alignment. Consequently, once the position of a cell on the path is known, two big blocks in the table are irrelevant: the one right above it and the one left below. The cells in these blocks need not be computed any more. Figure 2.6 illustrates this. Altogether, compared with the basic method, the computing time will roughly double: in the first step, we need to compute all the cells in the table. In the second, we need only about a half of them: the upper left and the lower right block. In the next step we compute only about a half of the cells in each block, approximately a quarter of

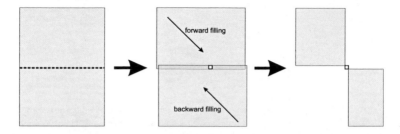

Figure 2.6: Divide-and-conquer strategy. In the first step, the empty table is split into two halves, overlapping in one row. Then, the above half is computed forward (top-down), and the lower backward (bottom-up). The last computed rows of both tables are added. The cell with the lowest distance (white square) is the cell on the optimal path and its position is stored. The path extends towards the top-left and bottom right corner, so the process is recursively repeated for the blocks where it can pass through.

the table, an so on. Altogether, the number of cells computed can be approximated by $mn \sum_{i=0}^{\infty} (1/2)^i = 2mn$. An exact derivation is given in (Wong and Chandra, 1976).

2.4.2 Speeding up the computation

The computational complexity of the above approach is still quadratic in the string lengths. However, at least a part of the computations is superfluous. Not only that the whole table need not be kept in memory, even computing all the cells is not necessary. Using a linear scoring scheme, the similarity score of a quadratic $n \times n$ table can never be below $-np$, corresponding to all symbols mismatched. Looking for a better score off the main diagonal never leads to a result better than $(n - w)p + 2wg$, which is obtained assuming $(n - w)$ matches and w gaps in each string. Therefore, the widest band for which it still makes sense to be searched is limited by the offset

$$w = \frac{2np}{p - 2g} \qquad (2.22)$$

from the main diagonal. For the usual values $p = 1$ and $g = -2$, w is $0.4n$. Considering that the number of table cells that has to be computed equals $N_C = 2nw - w^2$, it means that it is sufficient to compute 64% of the matrix to find the best alignment between two sequences. Graphically, the upper-right and lower left corner of the table need not be computed (for a more detailed discussion, see Kruskal and Sankoff 1983).

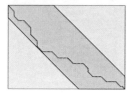

Figure 2.7: Reducing the computation time. If the path (dotted line) is known never to depart from the diagonal more than w cells, the computation can be limited to a diagonal band in the table.

This result can be generalized for rectangular $m \times n, m > n$ tables. Then, the optimal alignment must be searched off the main diagonal, since the longer sequence has to be aligned with some gaps. The band limits pass at $(m - n + w)$ below the main diagonal and w above it. The largest diagonal offset parameter w for which there is a chance of finding a better alignment than the worst possible is still given by Equation (2.22). For the usual values for p and g and taking into account that the number of cells in a rectangular matrix that needs to be computed is given by

$$N_C = mn - n^2 + 2nw - w^2 \qquad (2.23)$$

one never needs to compute more than $mn - (0.6n)^2$ cells.

The above estimate holds in the worst case, when all n symbols in the shorter sequence are mismatched with the n symbols in the longer sequence and the remaining $(m-n)$ symbols from the longer sequence aligned with gaps. In practice, the strings will usually share more similarities. It therefore makes sense to limit the search to a fixed-width band around the table main diagonal (Ukkonen, 1985), as depicted in Figure 2.7. This reduces the time complexity to $O(wm)$, w being the band width. The width can be chosen by the user, based on some prior knowledge about the string. If no such knowledge is available, one can start with a tight band and increase it gradually, until one finds the optimal path in the band. But how can it be known if the found path is optimal, i.e. that there exists no path outside the band leading to a better score? To be sure, one must compare its score with the theoretically best possible score of a path which exploits the whole band width. For a band with a width of w, such path contains w spaces, in order to exploit the whole band. The remaining symbols must produce a match, in order to achieve the highest possible score (the lowest distance). This score can be easily computed. If the score of the found path is higher than the best possible score exploiting the band width, one can be sure that the path is optimal.

If the strings differ much, this approach can lead to an *increase* of the computing time, because the same parts of the table – around the diagonal – have to be computed over and over again. The method is therefore useful only for similar strings. For arbitrary and very long strings (200000 symbols and more), the time complexity can be reduced to $O(n^2/\log(n))$ by trading some space for time (Masek and Paterson, 1980, 1983). In this work, such long strings did not appear, so this method was not used.

2.5 String averages

A distance measure for strings is sufficient for a nearest-neighbor classifier and for spectral clustering. Other methods, like self-organizing maps and learning vector quantization, also require a way to compute the mean of the data. This is straightforward for vectors, but not that easy for strings. The mean for vectors is simply their sum, divided by their number. Neither addition nor division are defined on strings.

2.5.1 Mean value for strings

For a vector space it is straightforward to show that the mean of a data set is the point with the lowest sum of squared distances (SSD) over the set:

$$\frac{\partial}{\partial\mu[j]}\sum_{i=1}^{N}(\boldsymbol{x}_i - \boldsymbol{\mu})^2 = 0$$

$$= -2\sum_{i=1}^{N}(x_i[j] - \mu[j]) = -2\sum_{i=1}^{N}x_i[j] + 2N\mu[j]$$

$$\Rightarrow \mu[j] = \frac{1}{N}\sum_{i=1}^{N}x_i[j] \qquad \text{for all } j \qquad (2.24)$$

Based on this observation, the mean can be generalized beyond vector spaces, as long as a distance measure is defined. Here it will be used to define a mean on strings. Contrary to vectors, where the mean is unique, many strings with the same, minimal SSD can exist for a set of strings. Take, for example, single-symbol strings A and B. Using unweighted edit distance, there are two strings satisfying the condition for mean: A and B. For larger sets and longer strings, the number of "means" can get so large that finding them all is not a realistic option. As it will be shown below, even finding one mean involves extensive computation. Therefore, taking this approach, we shall limit our aim at finding only one such string.

In this simple approach, the means were themselves members of the data set. This is generally not the case. For three strings AXCDE, ABYDE, and ABCZE, the fourth string ABCDE is the mean, with SSD = 3.

A simple idea for finding a mean string was proposed by Kohonen (1985) in context of speech recognition. Given a data set $\mathcal{D}$ consisting of strings, it starts by finding a string $s_m \in \mathcal{D}$ with the smallest sum of squared distances over the set. This string is taken as the first approximation of the mean, $\mu(0)$. In further steps, edit operations are performed systematically on it – replacements, insertions and deletions of all possible symbols at all possible positions – and checked if such an edited string is a better approximation of the mean, that is, if the sum of squared distances is reduced. The process is repeated until no single edit operation can reduce the distance.

Needless to say, this method is extremely inefficient and can be applied only on finite alphabets. Basically, it is an exhaustive search over all single edit operations. Even blatantly meaningless operations are performed, only to see that they actually increase the error and have to be undone. Having an alphabet Σ, $3|\Sigma|$ edit operations are tried out at each position, and there are $|\mu| + 1$ positions in the string. Finally, to compute the SSD, one needs to compare the modified μ with all $|\mathcal{D}|$ strings in the set.

The method of Kohonen (1985) relied not on an edit distance, but on the feature distance (Section 2.1). The feature distance, although having its above mentioned drawbacks, has also some practical advantages. In the context of a fixed data set, it suffices to find the string features (N-grams) only once and store them, say, in a hash table. In the subsequent iterations, when comparing the approximated mean with all strings, only the features of the mean have to be found after each modification. Comparing the strings can then be done relatively quickly, in time proportional to the number of distinct features in the mean string μ, because accessing the entries in the hash table has the time complexity $O(1)$. The number of features in the string depends on the string length, N-gram length and the alphabet size. For short strings, their number is proportional to the string length. As strings get longer, the possible combinations of N symbols eventually get exhausted, so the number of distinct features is $|\Sigma|^N$.

At the first glance, using edit distance leads to a higher computational effort. For two arbitrary strings of length n, computing the distance is $O(n^2)$. However, in applications in which string averages are normally used – K-means, SOM etc. – the strings in the set will usually be similar. In that case, it makes sense to use the above method for computing only the diagonal band of the dynamic programming table. This again allows a relatively fast string comparison. But, using edit distance, a significant speed-up in computing the mean can be achieved (Fischer and Zell, 2000a,b). The idea is to compute not only the distance between the μ-estimate and every string in $\mathcal{D}$, but also the whole edit transcript. As shown above, this can be done at asymptotically the same cost as computing the distance. Each edit transcript contains the operations needed to transform the μ-estimate into the corresponding data set string.

It is obvious that only operations that appear in the transcripts have a chance of reducing the SSD. Other edit operations make the μ-estimate not nearer to any other string and can only increase the sum of squared distances. Thus simply looking at the transcripts reveals which edit operations at every position make sense, and only these need to be tested when iteratively improving the μ-estimate. This already improves the performance. But, the idea can be pursued even further. The above described method computes the SSD directly, by comparing the μ-estimate with all set strings after applying each edit operation. This, however, includes a huge amount of redundant computation, because all but one position in the estimate remained unchanged. Or, put in other words, the optimal path through the dynamic programming tables changed only at one cell. The computation can be sped-up further if the number of comparisons is reduced, for example by performing them only after a number of edit operations have been applied. To be able to do this, we need answers to two questions: which operations to apply, and when to perform a new comparison with the set strings?

The heuristic proposed here is the following: For each position, find which edit operation is the most frequent in all transcripts. A "match" is also considered as an edit operation here, but with no effect on the string. Then, apply simultaneously the most frequent operation at every position. Compare the resulting string again with all set strings and repeat until the SSD cannot be further reduced. In other words, a majority vote is taken at each position in the string when choosing the best edit operation.

The heuristic, as presented here, does not actually lead to the minimum possible SSD. Applying the most frequent edit operation at a position in the mean string estimate reduces the edit distance by one for strings which "voted" for that operation, and which are in the majority. This, clearly, reduces the sum of distances over the set. But, for reducing the *squared* distances, in some cases it might be better to choose a less frequent operation. If some strings differ much from the estimate, modifying it towards them can reduce the sum of squared distances more than modifying it towards similar strings, even if the edit operation proposed by the similar strings overweighs. For example, consider the following three edit transcripts:

wbc	wbc	wbc
RMM	RMM	RRR
abc	abc	xyz

wbc is the current estimated mean string and the set of strings is $S = \{$ abc, abc, xyz $\}$. The estimated mean is not relevant for the discussion and is written only for convenience. For the first two strings, the transcripts contain only one non-match operation so the squared distance for each of them is one. The third string differs at all three positions, having the square distance of nine. For all strings, SSD $= 1^2 + 1^2 + 3^2 = 11$. At the first position in the transcripts, the most frequent edit operation is "replace by a". Applying it would make the mean identical to the first two strings and reduce the SSD by two. But, the operation "replace by x" is better. It leaves the distance between the mean and the first two strings unchanged, but reduces the distance to the third string from three to two. The SSD is thus reduced by five, to SSD $= 1^2 + 1^2 + 2^2 = 6$.

The above heuristic can be modified, for example by weighting the operations by the improvement in the SSD which they would produce. However, is this really necessary? If the aim is to obtain the string with the lowest SSD, the answer is obviously "yes". But, if the aim is to get a good representative of the string set, the answer depends on the data model. Minimizing squared distances is common for vectorial data, especially if the noise in them can be considered Gaussian. But strings are not vectors: strings can vary in length, whereas vectors have a fixed dimensionality. Also the symbols in strings are discrete objects and cannot be taken as analogous to vector components, and the noise cannot be Gaussian. Therefore, minimizing squared distances is not a guarantee to reach a good set prototype.

2.5.2 Median string

Edit distance bears some similarity to the Hamming and Manhattan distance, since it simply counts the edit operations – as opposed to the Euclidean distance, which sums the squared coordinate differences. This suggests that minimizing simply the sum of distances might be suitable for strings. For scalars, the measure with the minimal sum of distances over the set is the median. When the set size is odd, the median is defined as the middle element of ordered set members. Otherwise it is taken as the mean of its two neighboring elements. It is easy to see that the median has the minimal sum of distances. One only needs to build the set of distances between adjacent points, $\{d_{12}, d_{23}, d_{34}, \ldots, d_{N-1,N}\}$, and express the sum of distances over them. For the middle point $M = (N + 1)/2$, the sum is given by:

$$
\begin{aligned}
d_{12} \;+\;&\; 2d_{23} + 3d_{34} + \ldots + (M - 1)d_{M-1,M} + (M - 1)d_{M,M+1} + \\
+\;&\; (M - 2)d_{M+1,M+2} + \ldots + 2d_{N-2,N-1} + d_{N-1,N}
\end{aligned}
\tag{2.25}
$$

For any other point $Q < M$, the sum of distances is:

$$
\begin{aligned}
d_{12} \;+\;&\; 2d_{23} + 3d_{34} + \ldots + (Q - 1)d_{Q-1,Q} + (N - Q)d_{Q,Q+1} + \\
+\;&\; (N - Q - 1)d_{Q+1,Q+2} + \ldots + 2d_{N-2,N-1} + d_{N-1,N}
\end{aligned}
\tag{2.26}
$$

what is clearly larger than (2.25). The same holds for $Q > M$ and for even data set sizes.

Based on this observation, the generalized median can be defined: it is the point with the smallest sum of distances over the given set. For strings, the above heuristics can be applied for finding it, at least when no indels appear in the edit transcript. With indels present, the edit transcripts for different set strings can be of different lengths. In that case, positions in the transcripts do not correspond to positions in the median estimate, so choosing the most frequent operation at a position is not possible[2]. Observe, for example, the following transcripts:

```
a-c--f        acf         acf--
MIMIIM        DMM         MMDII
abcdef        -cf         ac-gh
```

The position (6) in the first transcript does not even exist in the other two. The problem is now to align the transcripts, which is equivalent to the problem of aligning the strings themselves. For two strings of length n, we have seen that it can be done in $O(n^2)$ time. Using conceptually similar dynamic programming algorithms as the above, N such strings could be aligned in $O(n^N)$ time, but this is not acceptable in practice. The problem itself is known to be NP-hard (Kececioglu, 1993, Wang and Jiang, 1994).

A number of heuristics exist for this problem. For the application of finding a prototype string, the *star alignment* (Altschul and Lipman, 1989) is a suitable choice, with known performance bounds (Gusfield, 1993). The idea is to start from one string – the "star center" – and align it successively with other strings. If an alignment results in insertions of spaces into the star center, these spaces are retained and such an extended string is used as the center for further alignments. In addition, spaces are simultaneously inserted into all previously aligned strings at the same position. In that way, the previous alignments with the center are preserved.

Having aligned all the set strings with the center, one can produce a new string by taking the most frequent symbol at every position. In molecular biology, such a string is called the *consensus string*. In counting, spaces in the alignments are also considered symbols, and are removed from the final string. It is obvious that such a string reduces the sum of distances over the set, at least when the edit operations carry the same cost. Otherwise, the symbols have to be weighted when computing their frequencies. The obtained string is not necessarily optimal, because star alignment is only a best-effort heuristic, depending on the initialization, that is, the choice of the center. However, by iteratively applying the alignment, using the string obtained in the previous iteration as the star center, a good approximate of the median can be reached.

---

[2]Needles to say, this problem also plagues the mean

2.5.3   On-line approximation of the string median

The above batch method is conceptually simple, but can be quite slow for a large number of strings. Also, it was mentioned in the Introduction (Section 1.3.2) that on-line pattern recognition methods can be considerably faster than their batch counterparts. To apply distance-based on-line algorithms on strings, we need a method for iteratively updating the prototype.

As a motivation, let us observe how the arithmetic mean can be computed in an iterative fashion for numerical data:

$$
\begin{aligned}
\bar{x}(t+1) &= \bar{x}(t) + \frac{1}{t+1} \left[x(t+1) - \bar{x}(t) \right] \\
&= \bar{x}(t) + \eta(t+1)\Delta(t+1).
\end{aligned}
\tag{2.27}
$$

where $\bar{x}(t)$ and $\bar{x}(t+1)$ denote the mean of the first t and $t+1$ input vectors, respectively, and $x(t+1)$ the input vector in the $t+1$-th iteration. Many pattern recognition algorithms, most notably self-organizing maps and learning vector quantization, use a simplified version of the above equation, in which $\eta(t)$ is a monotonuously decreasing function – not necessarily $1/t$, – as will be discussed in the following chapters.

Arithmetic operations, like addition and multiplication, are not defined on strings, so a direct analogy with Equation (2.27) is not possible. Instead, the following deliberation is relied on: what would happen if we would apply the star alignment algorithm not on the whole set, but only on a small subset? The obtained string would approximate the subset median, but not necessarily the set median. But, if the subset is representative for the whole set, the approximate would probably also not differ much from the set median. In any case, the approximate is not a worse star center than any other string, but probably better. Thus a good approximate of the set median can be reached by repeatedly computing the star alignment on a random subset, always using the result of the previous iteration as the star center.

The subset size can be fixed manually, as a user-defined parameter. But, its meaning for the results is not transparent to the user. What is a good size: 10, 100, or 10000 strings? What are the effects of the different sizes? To make the algorithm more user-friendly, it is preferable to have a measure related to the results. In this work, the statistical significance of the new approximation is relied on. For each position in the string, a simple binomial test for the two most frequent symbols is performed, again counting the spaces as valid symbols. The probability that the one is more frequent than the other only by chance is calculated. If the probability is below the user-defined threshold – the significance level, – the position is marked as stable. Otherwise, more strings are needed to make the decision, so further strings are taken into the subset.

Normally, not all positions will become stable simultaneously. The correct approach would be to keep collecting new strings into the subset, aligning them, and computing the significance. Once all positions are stable, the new star center is computed from the aligned strings. In practice, this has proven to lead to large sets, bringing no significant advantage compared to the batch method. Another approach is to apply changes at a position as soon as it becomes stable, and ignore this position in all strings already it the subset when calculating the significance in next steps. This approach is theoretically not correct, because, as the star center changes, the already computed alignment can change, too. Nevertheless, as experiments show, it leads to the correct mean with a high probability.

If weighted edit distance is used, it is not suitable to simply count the two most frequent symbols at each position and perform the binomial test. Instead, the symbols have to be weighted by the associated edit cost, and the two with the highest cumulative costs have to be compared. The zero-hypothesis is now that the both most weighted symbols carry actually the same cumulative weight, and that the observed deviation is due to randomness. If we denote the two highest cumulative weights by w_1 and w_2, the hypothesis is:

$$H_0 : p = \frac{w_2}{w_1 + w_2},$$ (2.28)

p being the probability of occurance of the more weighted symbol. If the hypothesis can be rejected at a user-specified significance level, the most weighted symbol is taken as the average symbol at that position in the string. Algorithm 2.1 presents the idea in pseudo-code.

The effect of the significance level is similar to the one of the parameter η in the numeric version: low significance, like high η, leads to more volatile approximations. The algorithm is not really an on-line one, because it waits to collect a certain number of samples before making any changes. But, it is even less a batch algorithm, since it does not need the whole data set to be available before making changes to the estimated median.

Figure 2.8 shows a comparison of the Kohonen (1985) algorithm for computing the string average with the here presented batch and on-line algorithm. As can be seen, both batch algorithms (the Kohonen algorithm is also a batch one) tend to be much slower than the on-line one as the set size rises. However, the algorithm presented here is still somewhat faster. But, the drawback of the Kohonen algorithm is even more obvious when the performance for different string lengts is considered. As the strings get longer (and in molecular biology, they can be hundreds of symbols long), the execution time rapidly rises. Already for modest strings of 50 symbols on average, the Kohonen algorithm is more than an order of magnitude slower than the here presented batch algorithm. The on-line algorithm brings an additional speed-up factor of about five. Also, the execution time

---

Algorithm 2.1: On-line approximation of the string average

1: Initialize string μ somehow, e.g. with a random string from the input set.
2: Initialize the star center: $\mu^* \leftarrow \mu$
3: **for** $i \leftarrow 1 \dots \text{len}(\mu)$ **do**
4:      **for all** $\alpha \in \Sigma$ **do**
5:          Initialize the weight of the symbol α at the position i: $w_{i\alpha} \leftarrow 0$
6:          Initialize the number of occurences of α at the position i: $n_{i\alpha} \leftarrow 0$
7:      **end for**
8: **end for**
9: **while** there are more strings in the input set **do**
10:     Take a string from the input set and put it into s
11:     Align it with the approximated mean: $(s, \mu') \leftarrow \text{align}(s, \mu)$
12:     $t \leftarrow \text{transcript}(\mu', \mu^*)$ // *start star alignment:*
13:     **for all** $\mathrm{D} \in t$ **do**
14:         Insert space at the corresponding position in μ^* and update indices of $n_{i\alpha}$ and $w_{i\alpha}$ accordingly.
15:     **end for**
16:     **for all** $\mathrm{I} \in t$ **do**
17:         Insert space at the corresponding position in s.
18:     **end for**   // *end star alignment*
19:     **for** $i \leftarrow 1 \dots \text{len}(s)$ **do**
20:         $\alpha \leftarrow s[i]$
21:         $n_{i\alpha} \leftarrow n_{i\alpha} + 1$
22:         $w_{i\alpha} \leftarrow w_{i\alpha} + p(\alpha, \alpha) - p(\alpha, \mu[i])$
23:     **end for**
24:     **for** $i \leftarrow 1 \dots \text{len}(s)$ **do**
25:         Find the most weighted α, β: $w_{i\alpha} \geq w_{i\beta} \geq w_{i\gamma}, \forall \gamma$
26:         Test the zero-hypothesis: $w_{i\alpha}$ and $w_{i\beta}$ both tend to the same value W as $n_{i\alpha}, n_{i\beta} \to \infty$
27:         **if** the hypothesis can be discarded on a user-specified significance level η **then**
28:             $\mu[i], \mu^*[i] \leftarrow \alpha$
29:             $w_{i\gamma}, n_{i\gamma} \leftarrow 0, \forall \gamma$
30:         **end if**
31:     **end for**
32: **end while**

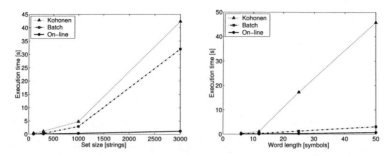

Figure 2.8: Speed comparison of string averaging algorithms, measured on artificial sets. **Left:** Execution time as a function of the set size. For the Kohonen and the batch algorithm, it rises much faster than for the on-line one, although the new batch algorithm is still better than the Kohonen's. **Right:** Execution time as a function of the average string length. For both algorithms presented here it rises only slowly, compared to the Kohonen's.

of the Kohonen algorithm rises with the alphabet size, whereas it remains almost constant for the other two algorithms.

The above comparison shows that the approximative, on-line algorithm is the fastest. But does it lead to good averages? In order to test this, a number of experiments have been performed. First, random sequences have been generated to serve as the original sequences. Algorithm 2.1 was used, but, instead of relying on a fixed set of corrupted strings, it was fed a new, on-the fly generated string in each iteration. The strings were obtained by corrupting the original sequence with noise. Despite a high level of noise, up to 75%, the algorithm in most cases converged to the original sequence. Even when it did not succeed, the sequence to which it converged was close to the original one. Table 2.1 summarizes the results.

In self-organizing maps, not only one prototype – the winner – is adapted, but also its topological neighbors, although, depending on the neighborhood function used, possibly to a less extent. For numerical data, this is easily achieved by scaling the difference between the prototype and the sample datum by the neighborhood factor τ (Equation (3.25)). For strings, the same effect can be achieved by weighting by τ. Also, in learning vector quantization, the prototypes of the class different from the sample datum have to be repelled from it. For numerical data, this is easily done by using a negative adaptation step. Analogously, when the prototypes are strings, the repulsion can be achieved by a negative weighting.

Table 2.1: Convergence of the on-line string averaging algorithm. Depending on the first approximation of the average (the initial star center) and the noise superimposed on the data, the algorithm converged to the original sequence in 62% – 97% of the cases. The noise level denotes the probability of edit operations at each position of the original sequence. The column **Iterations** shows the number of noisy strings presented to the algorithm before it reaches the original. The number of iterations was limited to 20000. If the algorithm did not converge, the last colum shows how often it converged to a similar string, within the specified Levenshtein distance.

Initial star center	Noise level	Converged	Iterations $\bar{n} \pm \sigma_n$	Converged within distance [%]				
				1	2	3	4	5
Original sequence	0.5	97%	796 ± 1294	3				
+ noise	0.75	80%	2759 ± 4945	15	5			
Random	0.5	89%	1678 ± 3337	3	3	1	0	2
sequence	0.75	62%	2639 ± 4658	16	10	7	1	2

Chapter 3

Distance-Based Unsupervised Learning

Unsupervised learning is mostly applied for gaining some insight into unlabeled data. The results of the learning are meant to be used directly by a human researcher. Sometimes a graphical data representation can be very useful and, for this reason, it makes sense to include some data visualization techniques into this chapter. By visual inspection, it is sometimes possible to directly determine clusters, however, an automated method is usually preferable, not only for its speed, but also for being probably less biased than a human. Both visualization and clustering methods described in this chapter rely strongly on a distance measure.

As a classical visualization method, Sammon mapping is presented. I will show below how the original algorithm can be improved and applied to strings when a distance measure is defined. K-means, a pure clustering algorithm relying on distance, is also presented and it is shown how can it be applied to strings. Finally, as a synthesis of clustering and visualization, self-organizing maps and their applications to strings are presented.

3.1 Data visualization: Sammon mapping

Data visualization is itself a large field and covering it in depth in a single thesis is not possible. Nevertheless, some issues concerned with high-dimensional and non-vectorial data are relevant for pattern recognition and are discussed here.

Graphically representing one- or two-dimensional vectors in a Cartesian coordinate system is the most straightforward possibility, easily done with a pencil and paper. With modern computers and graphics software, three-dimensional data can also be successfully visualized. From four dimensions on and for data other than vectors, more sophisticated techniques have to be used. If the data come from a metric space, the following idea can be pursued: Each datum is to be projected onto a lower-dimensional space (typically two-dimensional) in such way that the distances between the projections are as close as possible to the distances between the original points. If the input space metric correctly reflects the data structure, the structure remains preserved in the mapping. As a consequence, one can easily visually inspect the mapped vectors and infer properties of the original data: similarities, clusters etc.

Sammon's non-linear mapping (Sammon, 1969) is the earliest implementation of this idea and a number of improvements have been proposed, like distance mapping (Pekalska et al., 1999) or curvilinear component analysis (Lee et al., 2000), among others. However, the original Sammon's method still prevails in practice, and scientists can rely on a number of software implementations, many of them freely available (see, for example Kohonen et al., 1996, Murtagh, 1992, Venables and Ripley, 2001). The mapping has become an established tool in data analysis, with applications from document retrieval, as reported in the Sammon's original paper, to logo-therapy (Hatzis et al., 1996) and molecular biology (Agrafiotis, 1997), to name just few.

Let $\mathcal{X} = \{x_1, x_2, \ldots, x_N\}$ be the set of original data from a metric space. The distance between x_i and x_j shall be denoted by D_{ij}. Analogously, let $\mathcal{Y} = \{y_1, y_2, \ldots, y_N\}$ be a set of low-dimensional vectors, projections from $\mathcal{X}$. In the projection space, the Euclidean distance is used, and $d_{ij} = \|y_i - y_j\|$ denotes the distance between y_i and y_j. The task of the non-linear mapping is to compute the vectors from $\mathcal{Y}$ such that for all points, d_{ij} is as close as possible to D_{ij}. Ideally, $d_{ij} = D_{ij}$ should hold for every i and j, but this is obviously achievable only in exceptionally simple cases. To reach an approximate solution, Sammon proposed minimizing the following criterion:

$$E = \frac{1}{\sum_{i<j}^{N} D_{ij}} \sum_{i<j}^{N} \frac{(D_{ij} - d_{ij})^2}{D_{ij}} \tag{3.1}$$

E is the mapping error, often referred to as "stress". No assumptions are made about the distance function in the input space, making it suitable for any metric space. For mapping purposes the D_{ij}'s can be considered constants, thus the term $1/\sum_{i<j}^{N} D_{ij}$ is simply a constant scaling factor without influence on the mappings. It is nevertheless useful to incorporate it, for it normalizes the error with respect to the data set. This makes the mapping error on different data sets comparable.

It is obvious that the error is never negative and falls to zero when the $D_{ij} = d_{ij}$ for all pairs of input objects. Minimizing it is performed by choosing appropriate coordinates for vectors y_i. This is not a trivial task, but nevertheless a standard optimization problem. A great variety of numerical algorithms exists for that purpose. As a rule, they start from some initial (e.g. random) setting and iteratively adapt the vector coordinates. The procedure is repeated until the error cannot be further reduced.

The error function is a relatively simple continuous function, but not so simple that the minimum could be found analytically. Instead, a gradient descent method, like Newton's, can be used. The original Newton's method is an iterative method for finding a zero point of a non-linear function. In a simple, one-dimensional case, where the function depends only on one variable ($f = f(x)$), the method is described by the formula:

$$x(t+1) = x(t) - \frac{f(x(t))}{f'(x(t))} \tag{3.2}$$

where t denotes the iteration step. Basically, it approximates the function by a straight line and determines the next approximation of the zero-point as the point where the line intersects the x-axis. Recalling that function extremes are characterized by having the first derivative equal to zero, Newton's method can be applied as follows for finding them:

$$x(t+1) = x(t) - \frac{f'(x(t))}{f''(x(t))} \tag{3.3}$$

This approach, unfortunately, does not distinguish between a minimum and a maximum and leads to either one of them. An extreme is a minimum only if the second derivative is positive. Seeing that the second derivative appears in denominator of the above formula, we can try to force it to be always positive, thus "tilting" the direction of the adaptation step always towards minimum:

$$x(t+1) = x(t) - \frac{f'(x(t))}{|f''(x(t))|} \tag{3.4}$$

In case of Sammon Mapping, the error function – the function we wish to minimize – depends on many variables. Each coordinate q of every vector y_p influences it. The minimum has to be found by taking them all into account. The simplest (but not very good) approach is to treat them all independently and minimize the error along each of them separately. All this together leads to Sammon's adaptation rule:

$$y_{pq}(t+1) = y_{pq}(t) - \eta \cdot \Delta_{pq}(t) \tag{3.5}$$

η is an empirical "magic factor" which actually slows down the descent, but has a desirable effect of avoiding overshooting the minimum in highly non-linear areas. Typical values are between 0.3 and 0.4. Without loss of generality, we can set it to 1 and thus safely ignore it in further discussion. $\Delta_{pq}(t)$ is the adaptation step in the t-th iteration for the q-th component of an output vector y_p:

$$\Delta_{pq}(t) = \frac{\partial_{y_{pq}} E(t)}{\left| \partial_{y_{pq}}^2 E(t) \right|} \tag{3.6}$$

Here, a shorthand notation with the following meaning is used:

$$\partial_{y_{pq}} E(t) = \frac{\partial E(t)}{\partial y_{pq}} \quad \text{and} \quad \partial_{y_{pq}}^2 E(t) = \frac{\partial^2 E(t)}{\partial y_{pq}^2} \tag{3.7}$$

The form of the partial derivatives is not relevant for further discussion, but they are given here for completeness:

$$\partial_{y_{pq}} E(t) = \frac{-2}{\sum_{i<j}^N D_{ij}} \sum_{\substack{j \neq p}}^N \frac{D_{pj} - d_{pj}}{D_{pj} d_{pj}} (y_{pq} - y_{jq}) \tag{3.8}$$

and

$$\partial_{y_{pq}}^2 E(t) = \frac{-2}{\sum_{i<j}^N D_{ij}} \sum_{\substack{j \neq p}}^N \left[\frac{d_{pj}^2 - (y_{pq} - y_{jq})^2}{d_{pj}^3} - \frac{1}{D_{pj}} \right] \tag{3.9}$$

By considering the first error derivative to be locally linear, the method consequently assumes that the error function is locally quadratic. Then, if the second derivative is positive, the parabola is convex (facing upwards) and the adaptation step leads towards its angular point, which is also a (local) minimum. For a negative second derivative, the parabola is concave, but, thanks to taking the absolute value in the denominator, the adaptation step leads away from the angular point, which is in this case a local maximum.

3.1.1   Improving Sammon mapping

There are two problems with this simple approach. First, by simply taking the absolute value of the second derivative, Δ_{pq} is only guaranteed to have the optimal direction, but not size. When $\partial_{y_{pq}}^2 E(t)$ is negative, the above method assumes the minimum at the same distance but in the opposite direction of the estimated maximum. Put in other words, the error function is assumed to be antisymmetrical with respect to the current position. This can be true only by chance. In the vicinity of an inflexion point, the problem becomes even more serious: $\partial_{y_{pq}}^2 E(t)$ tends to be close to zero and causes Δ_{pq} to be very big. In the inflexion point itself, Δ_{pq} rises to infinity.

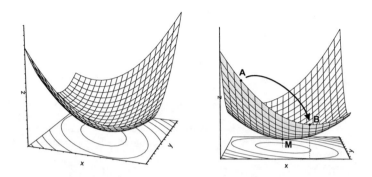

Figure 3.1: Finding the minimum of an elliptical paraboloid. **Left:** a percpective view of the paraboloid. **Right:** a view from the xz-plane. Starting from point A, the optimal adaptation of the x-coordinate alone leads to point B, which is the angular point of the parabola in the plane passing through A and being parallel to xz-plane. However, in search for the paraboloid minimum M, this approach overshoots it. The same holds for y-axis.

Another weakness lies in the simplification of Newton's method, by using the second derivatives only along coordinate axes. In other words, terms of type:

$$\frac{\partial^2 E(t)}{\partial y_{pq} \partial y_{uv}} \tag{3.10}$$

are ignored for all $p \neq u$ and $q \neq v$. Practically, this approach adapts all coordinates of a point independently of each other. Mathematically speaking, the Hessian matrix is supposed to be a diagonal one. It is easily seen that this assumption does not hold; off-diagonal elements are non-zero. As a consequence, the computed Δ_{pq} can be far away from the optimal one. The behavior is illustrated in Figure 3.1. It shows a hypothetical two-dimensional error function $z = E(x, y)$ from two slightly different viewpoints. In this example, $E(x, y)$ has a form of an elliptical paraboloid. On the left, a perspective view is given and on the right the function is shown as seen from the xz-plane (along the y-axis). Let us assume that the current approximation of the minimum lies at point A, with some coordinates (x_A, y_A, z_A). The actual minimum lies at M with coordinates (x_M, y_M, z_M). With Sammon's approach, adapting the x-coordinate of the current approximation would lead towards B – the point with the lowest z-coordinate at the fixed y. This

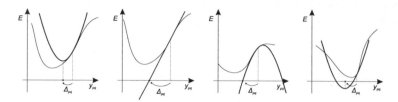

Figure 3.2: Four cases of error function shape and its quadratic approximation. From left-to-right: (1) error function is locally convex and the angular point of the approximation is above zero; (2) current minimum estimate is in the inflexion point and the parabola degenerates to a line; (3) concave error function; (4) convex error function and the angular point of the parabola is below zero.

point is the angular point of the parabola resulting from intersecting the paraboloid with the $y = y_A$ plane. It is obvious that this adaptation, although optimal for that y, overshoots x_M, which is the x-coordinate of the paraboloid minimum. By analogous reasoning it can be seen that the adaptation of y-coordinate is also wrong. Only by taking into account both axes simultaneously, the optimal step size can be computed.

A "minimally invasive" improvement would be to change as little as possible in the algorithm while fixing the weaknesses. The first weakness, arising from simply taking the absolute value of the error function's second derivative is easy to fix. Let us investigate four possible cases, illustrated in Figure 3.2. In the first case (extreme left), the parabola approximating the error function is convex and its angular point is above zero – this is the "normal" case for which Sammon's method works well. In the second case (center left), the current minimum approximation is in the inflexion point and the second derivative is zero. To avoid division by zero, which would happen in the Sammon's approach, we define $\Delta_{pq}(t)$ according to Newton's original method:

$$\Delta_{pq}(t) = \frac{E(t)}{\partial_{y_{pq}} E(t)} \tag{3.11}$$

In other words, we assume the error function to be locally linear.

In the third case (center right), when the parabola approximating the error function is concave, we choose the adaptation step to lead into the parabola's zero point:

$$\Delta_{pq}(t) = \frac{\partial_{y_{pq}} E(t)}{\partial^2_{y_{pq}} E(t)} + \text{sgn}(\partial_{y_{pq}} E(t)) \cdot \sqrt{\left(\frac{\partial_{y_{pq}} E(t)}{\partial^2_{y_{pq}} E(t)}\right)^2 - \frac{2E(t)}{\partial^2_{y_{pq}} E(t)}} \tag{3.12}$$

Finally, in the fourth case, the parabola is convex, but with the angular point below zero. Here, no obvious favorite exists and it is a matter of design which of the above three adaptation steps is chosen. Newton's rule is the most conservative, leading to smaller steps and consequently to slower convergence but also less oscillations, whereas jumping directly into the parabola's angular point is the most radical choice with opposite consequences.

This modified method works properly in all cases and needs only a minor modification of existing implementations, just a couple of lines of code. However, measurements show only insignificant improvements of convergence speed. It has to be concluded that the problem of Hessian matrix not being diagonal is the major one, so established optimization methods should be considered.

The method used by Sammon resembles roughly the Quickprop training algorithm for neural networks (Fahlman, 1988), with Quickprop being somewhat more heuristic and taking precautions in the above mentioned problematic cases. However, another method, Rprop (Riedmiller and Braun, 1993) (short for *resilient propagation*) performs better in many cases.

The key idea of Rprop is to use the error derivative only to determine the direction of the adaptation step. The step size depends on success of the previous iteration. It is computed according to a simple "reinforcement learning" rule: if the previous step left the gradient direction unchanged, the step size is increased. This has the effect of accelerating the descent in that direction. If the gradient direction changed, it is an indication that a minimum was jumped over. In that case, the direction is changed, and the step is reduced. In addition to these rules, the step size is limited from above and below to certain predefined values which are generally not critical for the performance. A big benefit of such behavior is that the step size remains reasonably large even in flat regions and reasonably small on steep slopes. This increases the convergence speed. At the same time, the risk of jumping far over the optimum is limited. While the first derivative of the error function appears only implicitly, the second derivative is not needed at all. This makes Rprop very easy to implement, because there is no need to compute the Hessian matrix.

The Rprop gradient descent rule is precisely described as follows:

$$y_{pq}(t+1) = y_{pq}(t) - \Delta_{pq}(t) \cdot \operatorname{sgn}\left(\partial_{y_{pq}} E(t)\right) \tag{3.13}$$

with

$$\Delta_{pq}(t) = \eta(t) \cdot \Delta_{pq}(t-1) \tag{3.14}$$

and

$$\eta(t) = \begin{cases} \eta^+ & \text{for} & \partial_{y_{pq}} E(t) \cdot \partial_{y_{pq}} E(t-1) > 0 \\ \eta^- & \text{for} & \partial_{y_{pq}} E(t) \cdot \partial_{y_{pq}} E(t-1) < 0 \\ 1 & \text{for} & \partial_{y_{pq}} E(t) \cdot \partial_{y_{pq}} E(t-1) = 0 \end{cases} \tag{3.15}$$

where

$$0 < \eta^- < 1 < \eta^+ \tag{3.16}$$

Typical values are $\eta^+ = 1.2$ and $\eta^- = 0.5$.
Based on these equations, Algorithm 3.1 is defined.

3.1.2   Comparison of mapping speed and quality

The two described variants of gradient descent (the modified rule for computing Δ_{pq} and the Rprop algorithm) have been tested in producing Sammon mappings of different real-world data sets. Two data sets from Murphy and Aha (1994), Iris (Fisher, 1936) and Pima Indians diabetes (Smith et al., 1988), contained numeric data. The third was constructed of amino-acid sequences of proteins belonging to the the kinases family, taken from the PIR data base (Barker et al., 1998). The results were compared with the results produced by original Sammon's algorithm. Three programs were written for this purpose: one, implementing the original Sammon's algorithm, the second one with the modified gradient descent and the third one with the Rprop algorithm. The programs were tested in a number of runs: 20 for the numerical data sets (Iris and Pima Indians) and 5 for the more complex kinases set. For better comparison, care has been taken that all programs use the same pseudo-random numbers in same runs. Table 3.1 summarizes the results.

As it can be seen, the Rprop algorithm is clearly superior to both the original Sammon's method and the modified version. For all data sets it is much faster, even orders of magnitude, and the resulting projections have significantly lower errors. The modified Sammon's gradient descent is roughly as fast as the original method, but in general leads to better projections. A lack of significant speed difference is not very surprising, because the algorithms share the same weakness concerning the Hessian matrix. However, it should be noted that in the 20 runs the original method diverged once on the Iris and twice on the Pima Indians data set, whereas both other methods are divergence-safe.

More sophisticated second-order methods, like conjugate gradient (Fletcher and Reeves, 1964) or Levenberg-Marquardt (More, 1977), are even more promising. It should be noted, however, that second-order algorithms are much more complex and consume much space and time on computing the Hessian. Measurements performed by my colleague Jan Poland suggest that Levenberg-Marquardt algorithm leads to a lower error, but, for larger data sets, at the price of slower computation. The Rprop algorithm is still orders of magnitudes faster.

Algorithm 3.1: Sammon mapping with Rprop gradient descent rule.

1: Let $\mathcal{X} = \{x_1, x_2, \ldots, x_N\}$ be the set of input data with a defined metric.
2: Let M be the dimensionality of the mapping space (normally two).
3: Initialize the projections $y_1, y_2, \ldots, y_N$ somehow, e.g. to random values.
4: **for** $p \leftarrow 1 \ldots N$ **do**
5:     **for** $q \leftarrow 1 \ldots M$ **do**
6:         Initialize the adaptation step Δ_{pq}: $\Delta_{pq} \leftarrow \Delta_{\text{INIT}}$
7:         Initialize the old partial derivative $\partial_{y_{pq}} E_{\text{OLD}}$ to zero.
8:     **end for**
9: **end for**
10: **for** $i \leftarrow 1 \ldots N$ **do**
11:     **for** $j \leftarrow 1 \ldots N$ **do**
12:         Compute the distance in the input space: $D_{ij} = d_{\text{IN}}(x_i, x_j)$.
13:     **end for**
14: **end for**
15: **while** the user-defined limit number of steps has not been reached **do**
16:     **for** $i \leftarrow 1 \ldots N$ **do**
17:         **for** $j \leftarrow 1 \ldots N$ **do**
18:         Compute the (Euclidean) distance in the mapping space:
$$d_{ij} = \sqrt{(y_i - y_j)^2}.$$
19:         **end for**
20:     **end for**
21:     **for** $p \leftarrow 1 \ldots N$ **do**
22:         **for** $q \leftarrow 1 \ldots M$ **do**
23:         Compute $\partial_{y_{pq}} E$ according to the Equation (3.8).
24:         Compute current η according to the Equation(3.15).
25:         Compute the new Δ_{pq}: $\Delta_{pq} \leftarrow \eta \Delta_{pq}$ (Equation (3.14)).
26:         **end for**
27:     **end for**
28:     **for** $p \leftarrow 1 \ldots N$ **do**
29:         **for** $q \leftarrow 1 \ldots M$ **do**
30:         Compute the new y_{pq}: $y_{pq} \leftarrow y_{pq} - \Delta_{pq} \text{sgn}(\partial_{y_{pq}} E)$ (Equation (3.13)).
31:         **end for**
32:     **end for**
33: **end while**

Table 3.1: Comparison of algorithms performance on different data sets.

Algorithm	Execution time (s) $\bar{t} \pm \sigma_t$	Projection error $\bar{E} \pm \sigma_E$
Iris data set (20 runs)		
Original	2083.6 ± 298.6	0.03344 ± 0.065
Modified	2004.7 ± 394.4	0.01233 ± 0.0027
Rprop	4.2 ± 4.24	0.00485 ± 0.0011
Pima Indians data set (20 runs)		
Original	60238 ± 1416	0.284 ± 0.077
Modified	57889 ± 11823	0.148 ± 0.088
Rprop	326 ± 184	0.013 ± 0.001
Kinases data set (5 runs)		
Original	71956 ± 1806	0.258 ± 0.08
Modified	72539 ± 2469	0.133 ± 0.021
Rprop	11269 ± 8100	0.045 ± 0.00005

3.2   Sammon mapping of string data

Sammon mapping is suitable as the first step in the analyisis of multi-dimensional or otherwise visually not representable data. It can be applied to string data, simply by defining D_{ij} in Algorithm 3.1 as a string distance.

The corrupted English words are not really an example of visually not representable data, since they can be written down and compared. But, as the excerpt from the data set shows (Section 1.5), the relationship between the words might still be hard to reveal.

Sammon mapping of the words (Figure 3.3) shows one approximately round cluster. The cluster is not homogenous, suggesting that more subclusters exist. As can be seen, words from the same class are mapped onto contigous areas. Nevertheless, without different markings for classes, it is not straightforward to say how many classes exist. As the noise level is increased, the overlap on the class boundaries also increases. Curiously, the classes can still be assigned a contigous area in the mapping.

A much different situation appears with the set of seven protein families (Figure 3.4). For some families, like sodium channel proteins, the dispersion inside the class is larger than the distance between other classes. Also, the mapping

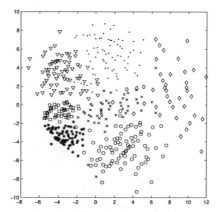

Figure 3.3: Sammon mapping for seven garbled English words. The words were garbled with 50% noise. The mapping produces a compact cluster, but classes are still well separated.

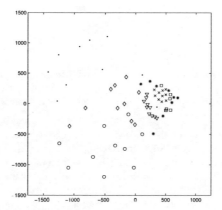

Figure 3.4: Sammon mapping for seven protein families. The fan shape is typical for poor mapping, when the mapping space cannot capture the relationships in the input space. Some classes are widely dispersed, whereas others are concentrated near one vertex of the "fan".

shows a typical fan shape, spreading angularly from one point. Such shapes are usually a sign that the mapping space is not rich enough to represent the data relationships. In this case, if the data were not labeled, it would be hard to tell if they form different clusters.

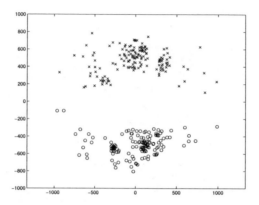

Figure 3.5: Sammon mapping for hemoglobine α and β chains. In the mapping, two clusters, corresponding to the two chains, are obvious.

For the hemoglobine data, the mapping is highly informative. Two elongated, slightly C-shaped clusters are obvious (Figure 3.5). Even more, a closer look suggests that the clusters split further in subclusters. One can guess the number of such subcluster to five or six.

Some structure can also be recognized in the mapping of kinase families (Figure 3.6). One family – the CMGC kinases, represented by diamonds, right on the map – forms a compact cluster, distinguishable from others. The PTK family (circles, on the left) could also be recognized, although not that easy, because at some points it touches the OPT family (crosses). OPT, containing various kinases not belonging to other families, is represented across the map, from top to bottom. Without it, it would be perhaps possible to differentiate between the AGC and CaMK families (triangles and squares), which are themselves quite near. There is also a slight overlap between the latter two families, at least in the mapping. Therefore, automated clustering methods, working directly on in the sequence space might be desirable.

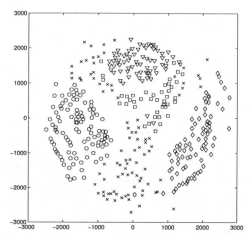

Figure 3.6: Sammon mapping of the kinase superfamily. The CMGC family (diamonds) and, somewhat weeker, the PTK family (circles) can be recognized as separate clusters. AGC (triangles) and CaMK (squares) families are not easy to separate. The picture is additionally complicated by the OPK family, which stretches accros the map.

3.3 Overview of clustering

The general assumption behind clustering is that the data form more or less identifiable groups (clusters), such that a certain degree of commonness is higher inside the groups than between them. Distance-based methods assume that the commonness is somehow reflected in the distance between data – the lower the distance, the higher the commonness. The primary task of clustering is to identify the data forming clusters, e.g. by enumerating them and listing all data belonging to the same cluster. Often, additional information are provided, for example: where are the cluster centers, what are their boundaries, which shapes do the clusters have, and so on.

The insight obtained by clustering can already be helpful by itself, but it can also support further processing steps. For example, a comprehensive summary about data, their distribution and shape can reveal relevant features and give clues about meaningful parameter settings for classification or about the applicability of different classification algorithms.

Many of the popular clustering algorithms consider clusters to be equal, in the sense that they compete each other. In other words, the data structure is considered flat. Another category are hierarchical algorithms: they assume data to form nested clusters, so each cluster can contain subclusters, each of them can contain further subclusters and so on. For certain applications, hierarchical clustering is a very natural representation and conceptually easy to understand. For example, relationships between species in biology are most naturally explained in terms of hierarchical families, subfamilies etc. Also, pattern recognition algorithms can be divided into three clusters: clustering, classification and function approximation algorithms; clustering consists of flat and hierarchical algorithms and so on. However, computational complexity of hierarchical algorithms is usually much higher than for the flat ones. Chapter 6 presents an algorithm that can be used for revealing the hierarchy.

An important and still largely unsolved question concerns the number of clusters to derive. Some algorithms, most prominently K-means, return a user-specified number of clusters, regardless of their validity. It is then the user's responsibility to specify a meaningful number. Another possibility is to rely on a criterion function. For example, one can take the criterion function of the form:

$$J_e = \frac{1}{N} \sum_{k=1}^{K} \sum_{x \in \mathcal{C}_k} d(x, \mu_k)^2, \tag{3.17}$$

where $\mathcal{C}_1, \mathcal{C}_2, \ldots, \mathcal{C}_K$ are the disjoint sets of points x, each represented by a μ_k. The criterion J_e can be minimized by choosing optimal K and μ_k's. The purpose is to minimize the quadratic deviation of the data from the cluster centers. Clearly, the minimum is reached when each datum is the center of its own cluster, since the distance would always be zero. A reasonable number of clusters can be found iteratively. The above criterion function falls monotonically with the increasing number of clusters, but beyond a certain value - the natural number of clusters - it falls only insignificantly. Such a function assumes spherical clusters and prefers clusters of similar sizes to diverse-sized clusters. Also, the choice of distance measure influences the outcome.

Other criterion functions can be defined, each having its own advantages and disadvantages. The main problem, however, is the computational complexity: the problem of finding the optimal partition is NP-hard (Garey and Johnson, 1979). There is an exponential number of possible partitions and an exact algorithm would have to check a large part, if not all of them in order to find the solution. Therefore, a number of heuristics have been proposed, aimed at achieving an acceptable computation time. The basic idea is to start with a reasonable guess for the number of clusters and their positions and to iteratively improve the values. Like all iterative approaches, this one is prone to local minimums. Other promising methods for estimating the number of clusters rely on spectral analysis of the data and are presented in Chapter 6.

3.3.1 Data distributions

In pattern recognition in general it is common to assume that the data are generated by some process which produces deterministic data, but, before reaching the observer, some noise is superimposed on them. In clustering, it is common to assume several processes, each generating a cluster. Lacking dependent attributes (they are present only in classification and regression), the noise can only influence the independent ones. For numerical data it is usual to assume a Gaussian noise, but in other cases, like for strings, other deliberations have to be made.

Having no previous knowledge, it is common to assume that all data generated by the same process are identical with a value, say, c_j. In other words, for each cluster there is a central (prototypical) point c_j from which the cluster points are obtained by superimposing noise to it. For numerical data this can be written as

$$\mathcal{C}_j = \{x_i, x_i = c_j + \xi_i\}$$

where ξ_i are samples from some random distribution and represent the noise. For non-numeric data, the influence of the noise has to be modeled in some other way, but the principle remains the same. In case of strings, the established approach is to model the noise as edit operations: replacements, insertions and deletions of symbols. The points c_j are referred to as cluster centers. Depending on the noise distribution they can, but need not coincide with the means of the cluster data.

Assuming clusters distributed around centers is the approach that imposes little structure on the data. For other cluster shapes, like numerical clusters distributed around lines, curves etc., the parameters of the shapes have to be determined, even if we knew which is the right shape. On the other hand, non-central clusters are not uncommon in real-world data. A number of models, traditionally most often regarded as neural, have been developed to counter this problem. The basic idea is to assume that each cluster, whatever shape it might have, consists of smaller, continuous areas where data distribution is homogenous and symmetric. For each of these areas, a separate representative is assigned. By connecting them, the whole cluster is covered. Details of specific models are discussed below.

3.4 K-Means

A classical and probably the best known distance-based clustering algorithm is K-means (MacQueen, 1967). This is a conceptually extremely simple hard-learning, iterative algorithm. It was originally stated as an on-line algorithm, but the batch version (Lloyd, 1982) is equally simple.

As the name suggests, K-means partitions the data into K clusters, each represented by its centroid (mean). The mean serves as the prototype or model value for the whole cluster. By clustering the data around cluster centers, K-means algorithm can be seen as a heuristics attempting to minimize the above criterion function (3.17). The original, on-line algorithm can be summarized as in Algorithm 3.2.

Algorithm 3.2: On-line K-means clustering

1: Let $\mathcal{D}$ be a set of data points x_i
2: Let $\mathcal{C}_j, j = 1, 2, \ldots, K$ be initially empty clusters.
3: **for** $j \leftarrow 1 \ldots K$ **do**
4:    Take a random point x out of $\mathcal{D}$ and put it into $\mathcal{C}_j$
5:    $\mu_j \leftarrow x$
6: **end for**
7: **while** there are more points in $\mathcal{D}$ **do**
8:    Take a random point x out of $\mathcal{D}$
9:    Find the corresponding cluster $\mathcal{C}_j : d(x, \mu_j) < d(x, \mu_k), \forall k \neq j$.
      In case of a tie, $d(x, \mu_q) = d(x, \mu_k)$ for some $q \neq k$, use $j = \min(q, k)$,
      i.e. the cluster with the lower index.
10:    Put x into $\mathcal{C}_j$.
11:    Compute the new μ_j: $\mu_j \leftarrow \text{mean}(\mathcal{C}_j)$.
12: **end while**

The tie-breaking criterion in Step 9 was formulated in (MacQueen, 1967). It is aimed at making the algorithm more "deterministic", i.e. delivering reproducible results if the data were presented in the same order. In practice, when points are picked randomly, the tie-breaking criterion is usually formulated as a stochastic one, assigning points randomly to equally distant clusters. Also, the mean in Step 11 is normally computed incrementally, according to the equation 2.27, so the clusters $\mathcal{C}_j$ need not be explicitly stored.

The algorithm is sensitive to the initialization and to the sampling order (Steps 4 and 8). The problem of sampling order can be alleviated by using the batch version of the algorithm. Instead of updating the centroids after every point is presented, it computes the new centroids as the means of all points being the nearest to the old ones. The process is repeated until all new centroids are identical with the old ones. The algorithm can be summarized as in Algorithm 3.3.

This algorithm is still sensitive to the initialization (Step 1). Both batch and on-line algorithm have another disadvantage: they prefer clusters of similar sizes. The more the clusters differ in size, the more striking the disadvantage. Consider the set $\mathcal{D} = \{0, 1, \ldots, 60, 70, 71, \ldots, 100\}$, i.e. integers from zero to 100 with the gap between 61 and 69. Obviously, the natural classification is into two clusters, $\mathcal{C}_1 = \{0, 1, \ldots, 60\}$ and $\mathcal{C}_2 = \{70, 71, \ldots, 100\}$. Their means are $\mu_1 = 30$ and $\mu_2 = 85$. But even using the correct means as initialization, the batch K-means

---

Algorithm 3.3: Batch K-means clustering

1: Let $\mathcal{D}$ be a set of data points x_i.
2: Let $\mathcal{C}_j, j = 1, 2, \ldots, K$ be initially empty clusters.
3: **for** $j \leftarrow 1 \ldots K$ **do**
4:     Take a random point x from $\mathcal{D}$.
5:     Initialize the cluster mean: $\mu_j \leftarrow x$.
6: **end for**
7: **repeat**
8:     **for** $i \leftarrow 1 \ldots N$ **do**
9:         Assign x_i to the corresponding cluster $\mathcal{C}_j : d(x, \mu_j) \leq d(x, \mu_k), \forall k$.
10:     **end for**
11:     **for** $j \leftarrow 1 \ldots K$ **do**
12:         $\mu_{j\text{OLD}} \leftarrow \mu_j$
13:         $\mu_j \leftarrow \text{mean}(\mathcal{C}_j)$
14:     **end for**
15: **until** $\mu_j = \mu_{j\text{OLD}}$ for all j

---

converges to $\mu_1 = 26.5$ and $\mu_2 \approx 79.8$, leading to the clustering $\mathcal{C}_1 = \{0, 1, \ldots, 53\}$ and $\mathcal{C}_2 = \{54, 55 \ldots, 60, 70, 71, \ldots, 100\}$.

Another reason why batch K-means leads to better results than the on-line version is that it makes several passes through the data set. It terminates only after reaching a stable state. This is in contrast to Algorithm 3.2, which makes only one pass through the set and does not necessarily reach a stable state. Therefore, the on-line algorithm is often extended to include more iterations through the set, as presented in Algorihtm 3.4.

Algorithm 3.4: Multi-pass on-line K-means clustering

1: Perform K-means according to Algorithm 3.2.
2: **repeat**
3:     **for** $j \leftarrow 1 \ldots K$ **do**
4:         $\mu_{j\text{OLD}} \leftarrow \mu_j$
5:     **end for**
6:     Perform Algorithm 3.2, starting from Step 7.
7: **until** $\mu_j = \mu_{j\text{OLD}}$ for all j

In the above simple, one-dimensional example, the question of cluster shapes did not make sense. In case of multi-dimensional data, the shapes can become an issue. Through its assignment rule, K-means implicitly expects the clusters to be spherical. More precisely, the underlying assumption is that the data distribution inside clusters is rotation invariant, i.e. that data density depends only on the dis-

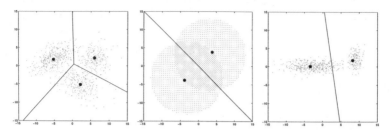

Figure 3.7: Three clusters found by K-means. Thick points denote estimated cluster centers and the lines the estimated cluster boundaries.

Figure 3.8: Two overlapping clusters. The centers estimated by K-means do not correspond to the real ones, which lie in the circle centers, but the boundary is correct.

Figure 3.9: Two elongated clusters. K-means is incapable of determining the correct boundary.

tance from the cluster center, and not on the direction. In case of the Euclidean distance measure, this corresponds to the common sense meaning of "round". Using the Mahalanobis distance, the algorithm implies elliptical clusters, and other distance measures lead to other presumed shapes. The cluster boundaries, however, are given by the Voronoi tesselation of their centers and are piecewise linear. They do not depend on the intra-cluster data distribution, but on the distribution of cluster centers in the data space. As a consequence, the shape of obtained cluster boundaries is not correlated to the real cluster shapes.

Figures 3.7-3.10 show examples of two-dimensional clusters and cluster boundaries obtained with batch K-means. As it can be seen, the cluster bound-

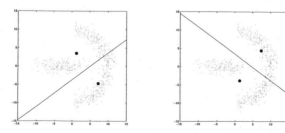

Figure 3.10: Results from K-means on the same data set but with different initial position of cluster centers. The class boundaries in the left and right figure are completely different.

aries, although not corresponding to cluster shapes, successfully enclose approximately round clusters, but, as Figure 3.8 shows, computed centers do not necessarily correspond to the real ones (± 3.8668 instead of ± 3.125). As the clusters get more elongated, or even concave, the obtained clustering departs from natural clusters. Figure 3.10 shows how different initializations can lead to significantly different results.

3.5 K-Means on string data

Both on-line (Algorithms 3.2 and 3.4) and batch (Algorithm 3.3) K-means can be applied to strings by using a string distance, like Levenshtein distance, or a similarity-based distance, as described in Section 2.3. In addition, an average for strings has to be used. K-means, as described above, use the arithmetic mean (Steps 11 and 13, respectively), but any other prototype is equally acceptable, if it adequatly represents the data relationships. As shown in Section 2.5.3, string medians can be computed significantly faster in an on-line manner. Therefore, Algorithm 2.1 was used in K-means for strings, implying the use of an on-line K-means algorithm. For better stability, multi-pass Algorithm 3.4 was used.

K-means with $K = 7$ was performed on the 50% corrupted English words, using Levenshtein distance. In a typical test, after 2000 iterations, the obtained set of prototypes was:

```
nce      railway    macrobiotics    underaged
woff     distance   philosopher
```

As can be seen, none of the obtained prototypes differs in more than one edit operation from the original word, used for generating the set. The quality of the results did not depend on the initialization. The dispersion of the strings is so high that even choosing an element from one cluster as the initial prototype did not guarantee that it will eventually converge to or come close to the real prototype for that class. The position of the prototypes in the Sammon mapping is shown in Figure 3.11. Also, the number of iterations is not critical for the perfomance, comparably good results have been achieved after 1000, 500, and even 300 iterations. Good results have been achieved even on the words corrupted by 75% noise:

```
ice      railway    macrobiotic    underaged
wols     distance   philosoher
```

Here, too, the obtained prototypes differ at most in one edit operation from the original words. There are three prototypes not identical to the original, compared

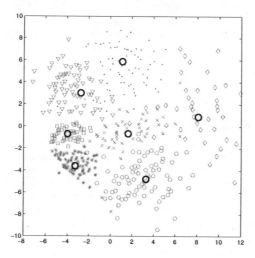

Figure 3.11: Sammon mapping of K-means for corrupted English words. Seven proto-types were used. The words were corrupted by 50% noise. Still, the prototypes are almost identical to the original, uncorrupted words.

to only two in case of 50% noise. Assignment of samples to clusters based on the prototypes is shown in Table 3.2.

Using 14 prototypes instead of seven lead to results like the following:

```
ice        railway       macrobitics       underaged
wolf       distance      philosopher       uneahd
mcrblotias               hsosopher
jhinvofpzepi             micrflbotxhercsv
phpqzwosopjern           mcceobdiojjrzxcs
```

As it can be seen, some prototypes converged towards the original words, whereas others seem completely uncorrelated with them. The former actually represent the clusters, while the latter cover only distant outliers. In the mapping (Figure 3.12), the prototypes are pushed away, to the outer frontiers of the set.

For clustering biological data, a distance measure based on BLOSUM62 scor-ing matrix was used. For the hemoglobine chains, already two prototypes suffice to separate the data into the natural clusters, α and β chains: 164 samples are assigned to the α cluster and 157 to the β cluster. The numbers sum to 321 – one more than the set size – because one sample is equally near to both prototypes and can be assigned to any of the clusters. In practical application, one could resolve

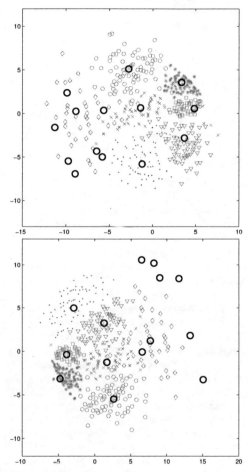

Figure 3.12: Sammon mapping of K-means for corrupted English words, with 14 prototypes. **Above:** Mapping for the data with 50%-noise. **Below:** Mapping for 75% noise. The superfluous prototypes are pushed aside, seven or eight are sufficient for representing the data.

Table 3.2: K-means of corrupted English words, using seven prototypes. Each prototype covers a a cluster quite well. Short words, `ice` and `wolf` are less specific and are more likely to be confused. This lies on the Levenshtein distance used, which punishes each edit operation equally.

	μ_1	μ_2	μ_3	μ_4	μ_5	μ_6	μ_7
ice					60		
wolf	74				13		
railway	3			48	5		
distance			65		8		
underaged	4		1	2	7		74
philosopher	3	77	1		2		
macrobiotics	1	1				40	

the ambiguity by assigning it randomly to only one cluster. The same clustering results were obtained in different runs and with different parameters, independent of the initialization.

It was said in Section 3.2 that one can recognize five or six clusters in the Sammon mapping of the hemoglobine data. Performing K-means on them with six prototypes leads to results like in Table 3.3. Contrary to the expectations, the algorithm is able only to recognize the two large clusters, α and β. Most of the data in the set are represented by only two prototypes, one for each family. The remaining prototypes cover only single outliers. A graphical representation is given in Figure 3.13.

The above results have been obtained using relatively volatile prototypes, at the significance level $\eta = 0.2$. But even with a more conservative approach, with $\eta = 0.02$, the distribution of prototypes is only slightly better (Table 3.4). They still do not cover the natural subclusters, corresponding to A- and D-type of the α-chain and different species (mammals versus others) in the β-chain. The number of samples covered by each prototype corresponds roughly to the number of sub-cluster members, suggesting that the differentiation might work to a certain extent (Table 3.4). However, looking more closely which data are covered by which prototype, it is obvious that the correspondence is not very reliable. Moreover, the results are not reproducible, leading to quite different results in different runs (Table 3.5).

K-means was applied to the kinase data set using five and ten prototypes, and in with $\eta = 0.02$ in both cases. Again, BLOSUM62 scoring matrix was used. As Table 3.6 shows, four classes are quite well represented by the prototypes, only the OPK class is covered by several prototypes. The reason for this apparent

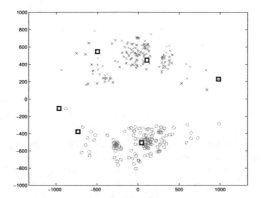

Figure 3.13: K-means for two hemoglobine chains. The prototypes are mapped on the original Sammon map of the proteins. Six prototypes were used, but already two cover almost the whole set.

Table 3.3: K-means of hemoglobine α and β chains using six prototypes and $\eta = 0.2$. μ_i are the prototypes, and N_α and N_β denote the number of sequences from each class that are assigned to the prototype. Already two prototypes, μ_3 and μ_5 represent almost the whole set divide in into the correct classes. One string is equally near to two prototypes, therefore the numbers in the table sum to 321, which is one more than the set size.

	μ_1	μ_2	μ_3	μ_4	μ_5	μ_6
N_α		1	159			4
N_β	1			2	154	

Table 3.4: K-means of hemoglobine α and β chains using six prototypes and a more conservative $\eta = 0.02$. Number of samples covered by each prototype suggests that there might be subclusters in each cluster.

	μ_1	μ_2	μ_3	μ_4	μ_5	μ_6
N_α	5			33	103	23
N_β		44	113			

Table 3.5: K-means of hemoglobine α and β chains using six prototypes and $\eta = 0.02$. **Above:** Correspondence of the data to the five natural clusters, based on the same prototypes as in Table 3.4. The prototypes $\mu_2 - \mu_6$ seem each to cover a cluster, although the clusters α-3 and β-2 are not well expressed. **Below:** The same clustering based on prototypes from another run. The prototypes μ_1 and μ_5 split one cluster among themselves, whereas μ_3 covers both β clusters.

	μ_1	μ_2	μ_3	μ_4	μ_5	μ_6
$N_{\alpha 1}$	5				91	
$N_{\alpha 2}$				30	3	
$N_{\alpha 3}$				3	9	23
$N_{\beta 1}$			100			
$N_{\beta 2}$		44	13			

	μ_1	μ_2	μ_3	μ_4	μ_5	μ_6
$N_{\alpha 1}$	72				24	
$N_{\alpha 2}$	3			30		
$N_{\alpha 3}$	11	21				4
$N_{\beta 1}$			100			
$N_{\beta 2}$		2	56			

Table 3.6: K-means clustering of five kinase families using five prototypes. All families except OPK are well represented.

	μ_1	μ_2	μ_3	μ_4	μ_5
AGC	2				69
CMGC		80		1	
CaMK	42				
PTK			104		
OPK	9	3	33	48	1

Table 3.7: K-means clustering of five kinase families, using ten prototypes. Compared with the clustering with $K = 5$, the ACG family remained unchanged, CMGC, CaMK and PTK are split into two as the number of prototypes is increased. No regularity can be observed for the OPK class.

	μ_1	μ_2	μ_3	μ_4	μ_5	μ_6	μ_7	μ_8	μ_9	μ_{10}
AGC						69	2			
CMGC					10		1			70
CaMK			30				12			
PTK		46							58	
OPK	4			1		1	63	6	15	2

anomaly is that OPK (*other* protein kinases) is not a compact class itself, but only a convenience label for all kinases not belonging to any of the other four families (see Figure 3.14). The clustering is reproducible, only the classification of the OPK class changed in different runs. In the example shown in Table 3.6, the prototype μ_4 covers a relative majority of the OPK family, but a considerable number of sequences from it are dispersed among other clusters.

Using ten prototypes instead of five did not change the clustering much (Table 3.7). The most important difference is that the PTK family was split into two subclusters. Also, the CMGC family was split into a bigger cluster, of 70 samples, and a smaller one, consisting of only 10 samples. Occasionally, the CaMK family was split in two subclusters, of 30 and 12 samples, like in this example. In other runs, it remained one cluster, as in the case when only five prototypes were used. In all cases, the OPK family behaved "greedy", consuming as many prototypes as it could.

For the seven hand-picked protein families, already the Sammon mapping suggested that it will be hard to cluster them. In the mapping itself it was not possi-

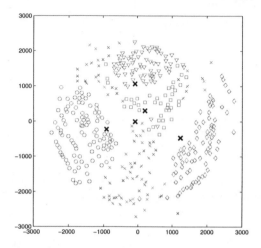

Figure 3.14: K-means for the kinase families, with $K = 5$. The prototypes are mapped on the original Sammon map of the proteins. They are well dispersed over the set and one can be identified for each family except for the OPK.

ble, but it could be possible in the original, string space. Unfortunately, this hope could not be substantiated. For K-means, the whole set appeared to be one very dispersed cluster. Only a couple of prototypes cover much of the data, regardless of their class membership. In a typical run, presented in Table 3.8, one prototype covered a large part of the set, with elements from six out of seven available classes. Most of the remaining prototypes covered only a single or a pair of data. Similar results were obtained using ten and seven prototypes and with different significance levels η.

3.6   Self-organizing maps

In the beginning of this chapter, Sammon mapping was presented as a possibility for visualizing high-dimensional or non-vectorial data. The mapping itself performs no clustering, but the clusters can be determined manually by inspecting the visualization. On the other extreme are the clustering methods like K-means. They provide for no visual representation of the data and their results have to be taken as they are.

The self-organizing map (SOM) (Kohonen, 1982, 1995) is in a sense a combination of both: it processes data in a way similar to K-means and at the same

Table 3.8: K-means clustering of seven protein family samples, using 15 prototypes, μ_i. N_i is the number of elements from the i-th class assigned to the prototype in the corresponding column. The clustering is poor, one prototype covers a large part of the set, two others somewhat smaller parts, and the remaining prototypes cover each only a couple of strings.

	μ_1	μ_2	μ_3	μ_4	μ_5	μ_6	μ_7	μ_8
N_1	10							
N_2	5							
N_3	6							
N_4	1				3		1	
N_5		1	1			1		2
N_6	1			2				
N_7	4							

	μ_9	μ_{10}	μ_{11}	μ_{12}	μ_{13}	μ_{14}	μ_{15}
N_1							
N_2						5	
N_3						2	
N_4	1				4		
N_5				3	2		
N_6		5	1			1	
N_7						1	5

time it performs a dimensionality reduction, allowing for the visual representation of the data. Since its introduction in the early 1980s it has enjoyed a huge popularity. Historically and by its motivation, it has been considered a neural model and, together with the multi-layer perceptron, it is today probably the best known artificial neural network. In the context of this thesis, the biological motivation is of secondary importance. It suffices to say that it has been observed in animal brains that certain structures (cortical columns) that are physically close also tend to react to similar stimuli (see Kohonen, 1995, Ritter et al., 1990). By the analogy, the SOM attempts to produce a data abstraction such that adjacent areas in the map correspond to similar points.

From a pattern-recognition point of view, a motivation can be derived from the following consideration: It was shown above that K-means implies spherical clusters. Parametric methods, like those used in connection with expectation-maximization, also assume some specific cluster forms, in detail controlled by the parameters. If the assumptions are wrong, the clustering produces not the natural clusters, but artifacts. Without specific knowledge about the data, it is preferable to have the assumed form as flexible as possible. One possibility is to try to approximate the clusters by some kind of a grid. For the flexibility, the number of nodes should be significantly higher than the number of expected clusters. In order to achieve a good abstraction and cancel noise, it should also be much lower than the number of points in the data set.

In order to form the grid, two questions have to be answered: how to position the nodes, and how to connect them. For positioning, it is again useful to assume some probability distribution behind the data. In a sufficiently small vicinity around every point in the input space, we shall assume that the data density can be considered constant. In the vicinity C with the volume $V(C)$ around some point x, the density $p(x)$ can be expressed as

$$p(x) \approx \frac{P(x \in C)}{V(C)}. \tag{3.18}$$

The probability $P(x \in C)$ can be approximated by the fraction of sample points in the cell:

$$P(x \in C) \approx \frac{n_C}{N} \tag{3.19}$$

where $n_C = |\{x_i : x_i \in C\}|$ denotes the number of points sampled in the cell C. A further simplification is to quanitize the probability $P(x \in C)$ to an integer multiple of some elementary probability:

$$P(x \in C) \approx kq, \quad k \in \mathbf{N}_0 \tag{3.20}$$

with $q = M/N$ and $k = \lfloor n_C/M \rfloor$, where $M \in \mathbf{N}, M < N$ is some user-defined constant which determines the coarsness of the approximation. Simply put, the elementary probability q represents always M samples from the set. Understanding each node in the grid as a carrier of the elementary probability, the data distribution is approximated by placing k nodes into corresponding cell $\mathcal{C}$.

To form the grid, the nodes have to be connected somehow. A plausible requirement is to connect only adjacent nodes. Also, for visualization purposes it is usefull for the grid to form a planar graph (at least for the two-dimensional map, which is most common in practice). SOM adaptation algorithm is a best-effort heuristics for that purpose. It actually starts from the back, fixing the mapping as a low-dimensional grid and then adapting its nodes so that they reflect the data density. Typically, in two dimensional maps, regular triangular and rectangular grids are used, although other forms and even irregular grids are also possible. In one-dimensional mapping, the nodes are connected into a chain. The connections are fixed, only node positions in the input space are changed during training. The adaptation of nodes resembles K-means: for each sample point, the nearest node is attracted towards it. In SOM terminology, derived from competitive learning, such a node is called "winner". In addition, the neighboring nodes are also attracted in the same direction, to a degree depending on their map distance from the nearest node. It is important to note that "neighborhood" here refers to the mapping, not to the input space! Two nodes are considered immediate neighbors if they are directly connected by an edge in the grid. Their distance in the input space is irrelevant.

There are various ways of defining the topological (map) distance. In case of the rectangular grid, one possibility is to take the larger of the column and row distances. This way, all nodes having the same distance from a fixed node μ lie on the edges of a square centered at μ. Another possibility is to use Euclidean distance on the map, putting the nodes with the same distance on a circle. For the triangular grid, as originally proposed by Kohonen, the largest of the distances along three axes is taken. In such grids, nodes with the same distance from the winner lie on the edges of a hexagon.

Like in K-means, in the input space any metric d can be used for determining the winner node:

$$w = \arg\min_i d(\boldsymbol{\mu}_i, \boldsymbol{x}) \tag{3.21}$$

This makes SOMs applicable to non-vectorial data, including symbol strings. The amount by which the winner is moved towards the data point depends on the distance between the two and on the parameter η, called *learning rate*. The learning rate is a real number, $0 < \eta < 1$ and is continuously decreased during training. It is therefore more correctly denoted by $\eta(t)$, t being the iteration step, or the time since the beginning of the training. It is common to start with a value for η close to one and decrease it towards zero by the end of the training. In this way, the winner approaches the mean value of the points in its input-space vicinity, scaled by some constants, which depend on the decay process of η. For exact proof, see (Kohonen, 1995).

For the winner's topological neighborhood, one more factor determines the adaptation step size. This factor, which shall be here called the "proximity factor" and denoted with τ, is actually a function of the topological distance from the winner node. For the distance equal to zero (i.e. the winner node itself) it has a value of one and for topologically distant nodes a value approaching or equal to zero. A very simple such function is the so-called "bubble" neighborhood:

$$\tau\left(d_T(\boldsymbol{\mu}_w, \boldsymbol{\mu})\right) = \begin{cases} 1 & \text{for } d_T(\boldsymbol{\mu}_w, \boldsymbol{\mu}) < r \\ 0 & \text{otherwise} \end{cases} \tag{3.22}$$

Here, d_T denotes the topological distance function between the node $\boldsymbol{\mu}$ and the winner node $\boldsymbol{\mu}_w$, and the parameter r is the neighborhood radius. Somewhat smoother is the conical function:

$$\tau\left(d_T(\boldsymbol{\mu}_w, \boldsymbol{\mu})\right) = \begin{cases} 1 - \frac{d_T(\boldsymbol{\mu}_w, \boldsymbol{\mu})}{r} & \text{for } d_T(\boldsymbol{\mu}_w, \boldsymbol{\mu}) < r \\ 0 & \text{otherwise} \end{cases} \tag{3.23}$$

Another, even smoother and very popular proximity function is the Gaussian:

$$\tau\left(d_T(\boldsymbol{\mu}_w, \boldsymbol{\mu})\right) = \exp\left(-\frac{d_T(\boldsymbol{\mu}_w, \boldsymbol{\mu})^2}{2r^2}\right) \tag{3.24}$$

Like the learning factor, the neighborhood radius is decreasing with time – this corresponds to using ever smaller cells for density estimation. Thus it should be precisely denoted by $r(t)$ and, consequently, the proximity function as $\tau\left(d_T(\boldsymbol{\mu}_w, \boldsymbol{\mu}), t\right)$. Kohonen suggests starting with a large radius, even larger than half of the map diameter, and decreasing it towards one or zero.

Altogether, when presented a point $\boldsymbol{x}$, the adaptation step for the node $\boldsymbol{\mu}_i$ at the time instant t can be written as:

$$\Delta\boldsymbol{\mu}_i(t) = \eta(t)\tau\left(d_T(\boldsymbol{\mu}_w, \boldsymbol{\mu}_i), t\right)(\boldsymbol{x} - \boldsymbol{\mu}_w) \tag{3.25}$$

where $(\boldsymbol{x} - \boldsymbol{\mu}_w)$ is the difference in the input space between the sample point $\boldsymbol{x}$ and the winner node $\boldsymbol{\mu}_w$. The learning rate η and the proximity function τ are often considered together and concisely denoted by $h_{wi}(t)$. Thus the iterative SOM update rule can be briefly written as:

$$\boldsymbol{\mu}_i(t+1) = \boldsymbol{\mu}_i(t) + \Delta\boldsymbol{\mu}_i(t) = \boldsymbol{\mu}_i(t) + h_{wi}(t)(\boldsymbol{x} - \boldsymbol{\mu}_w) \tag{3.26}$$

provided addition and subtraction are defined in the input space. This rule is actually a simplified, but still analogous rule to Equation (2.27).

Graphically, one can imagine a two-dimensional SOM as a flexible and stretchable net, being bent and stretched and laid in a higher, e.g. 3-dimensional input space, in order to cover data points there. The one-dimensional SOM is even easier to imagine: it can be seen as a stretchable and flexible string with knots on it, laid in a higher-dimensional space so that the knots are concentrated in areas with a high data density. The training can be seen as taking randomly a point from the input space, finding the nearest knot in the SOM and drawing it a bit towards the point. As the knot is drawn, it tows the neighboring knots in the SOM. The process is repeated with decreasing the stiffness of the SOM and the adaptation step size.

More exactly, the whole SOM training algorithm is presented in Algorithm 3.5.

Algorithm 3.5: On-line SOM adaptation algorithm

1: Initialize the prototypes μ_i somehow (e.g. randomly) and assign each a unique position in a low-dimensional grid (map).
2: Initialize r and η to some values $r(0)$ and $\eta(0)$.
3: **while** the number of iterations is below some user-specified limit **do**
4:     Take a random point x from the data set $\mathcal{D}$
5:     Find the winner prototype $\mu_w : w \leftarrow \arg\min_i d(\mu_i, x)$ (Equation 3.21).
6:     Update the nodes in the map:
    $\mu_i(t+1) = \mu_i(t) + h_{wi}(t)(x - \mu_w)$ (Equation 3.26).
7:     Reduce the neighborhood radius r and the learning factor η.
8: **end while**

According to Kohonen, it is not very important how r and η are reduced. A very simple and effective approach is to reduce them linearly towards zero. Another common approach is exponential decay. This way r and η approach zero asymptotically, fast in the beginning of the training and slow towards the end. In both cases the nodes approach the weighted means of data in their neighborhoods, the weighting depending on the size and form of the topological neighborhood, controlled by the factor τ. The question that logically comes up is the following: if the nodes are intended to be the means of the neighborhoods, why not computing them explicitly as such, instead of relying on an iterative approximation? The batch variant of SOM does exactly that. Each prototype is computed as:

$$\mu_i(t+1) = \frac{\sum_j x_j \tau\left(d_T\left(\mu_w(x_j), \mu_i(t)\right), t\right)}{\sum_j \tau\left(d_T\left(\mu_w(x_j), \mu_i(t)\right), t\right)} \tag{3.27}$$

where $\mu_w(x_j)$ denotes the winner node for x_j. The whole algorithm is described in Algorithm 3.6.

The batch SOM is reportedly more stable and less sensitive to initialization than the on-line version. Like other batch algorithms, it has the drawback of being considerably slower than its on-line counterpart.

Algorithm 3.6: Batch SOM adaptation algorithm

1: Initialize the prototypes $\boldsymbol{\mu}_i$ somehow (e.g. randomly) and assign each a unique position in a low-dimensional grid (map).
2: Initialize r to some value $r(0)$.
3: **while** the number of iterations is below some user-specified limit **do**
4:    **for all** $x \in \mathcal{D}$ **do**
5:       Find the winner prototype $\boldsymbol{\mu}_w : w \leftarrow \arg\min_i d(\boldsymbol{\mu}_i, \boldsymbol{x})$ (Equation 3.21).
6:    **end for**
7:    Update the nodes in the map according to Equation (3.27).
8:    Reduce the neighborhood radius r.
9: **end while**

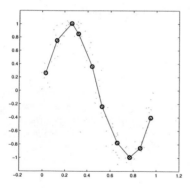
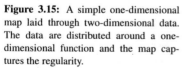
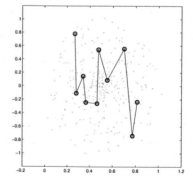

Figure 3.15: A simple one-dimensional map laid through two-dimensional data. The data are distributed around a one-dimensional function and the map captures the regularity.

Figure 3.16: The same map as in Figure 3.15 is laid through two-dimensional data distributed along both dimensions. The map cannot capture the regularity.

A disadvantage shared both by batch and on-line SOM lies in the map dimensionality that has to be fixed in advance. It has been said above that the SOM can be seen as a flexible, stretchable grid being laid in a higher-dimensional space to cover the data. This works well if the inherent data dimensionality roughly corresponds to the map dimensionality. For example, a two-dimensional SOM can nicely cover data in a higher-dimensional space if they lie around a two-dimensional surface in that space. Each point on the surface can be described by a function of two parameters and each node in the map is described by its row and column coordinate, so the correspondence between the surface and the map can be established. If the inherent data dimensionality is higher than the map dimensionality, the map becomes "crumpled", projecting similar data to distant parts of the map. Figure 3.15 shows an example of a data successfully approximated by a one-dimensional SOM. The data were generated by adding noise to a sine function. An opposite example is shown in Figure 3.16: the data are dispersed uniformly along both axes, so a one-dimensional SOM fails to suitably represent them.

At this point one could wonder what is exactly meant by a suitable representation? Can it be quantified somehow? Different measures have been proposed (see Bauer and Pawelzik, 1992, Villmann et al., 1997), mostly being more complicated to compute than the map itself. Also, the SOM learning algorithm is a stochastic one, depending on the initialization and the order how points are presented, so it is interesting to know how likely it is to converge to a good solution. Convergence has been proven in some special cases, e.g. one-dimensional maps, but no general proof exists. If one could express the SOM state in terms of some criterion ("energy") function, gradient descent methods could be used for minimizing it. However, in case of continuous distribution of input data, no energy function can be defined on the original SOM (Erwin et al., 1992). This disadvantage can be overcome by a slight modification of the SOM learning algorithm (Heskes, 1999), but it has been seldom used in practice. Obviously, despite all disadvantages, the original SOM is still appealing for its simplicity and effectiveness.

3.7 Self-organizing maps applied to strings

Whereas Sammon mapping shows the original points projected onto a lower-dimensional space, self-organizing maps perform one more level of abstraction, showing the local prototype data. They can be applied to strings in using the same distance measures and the the method for computing the prototypes as in K-means.

The first known self-organizing map for strings was published by Kohonen and Somervuo (1998). It was a batch map, and the training algorithm relied on feature

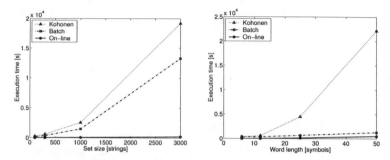

Figure 3.17: Speed comparison of SOM for strings, measured on artificial sets. Like for the string averaging algorithm (Figure 2.8), the on-line algorithm is the fastest, both with respect to set size (**left**) and to string length (**right**). The batch algorithm used here is slightly better the Kohonen's one with respect to the set size, but significantly better when long strings are involved.

distance (Section 2.1) and used the exhaustive search algorithm for computing the average. The algorithm could be significantly accelerated by using the averaging Algorithm 2.1 and implementing the whole map as an on-line one. A simplified version of Algorithm 2.1 is suitable for batch SOM, still being faster than the Kohonen's, but not as fast as the on-line map (Figure 3.17).

A highly illustrative example is the SOM of the seven corrupted English words (Figure 3.18). Although the map was initialized with random strings from the data set, randomly distributed over the map, after only 200 iterations the map converged to a state with clearly defined areas for each word. All seven original words are successfully reconstructed and assigned convex areas in the map. Most of the map nodes correspond to the original words. Only at class boundaries, artificial transition words appear. The map was produced using the "bubble" neighborhood function, with the initial radius $r = 3$, linearly reduced to zero, and with a constant $\eta = 0.02$. Comparable results were also obtained with higher values for η (up to 0.2), but after more iterations, typically 500 to 1000.

For the seven protein families, the results are better then one might expect. Although the set is hard to visualize and to cluster by K-means, the SOM converges to a state where different areas can be clearly recognized as sharing a degree of similarity. Figure 3.19 shows the map in two states: shortly after the beginning, when the neighborhood radius is still large and the nodes represent widely different strings, and after 7500 iterations (the initial state is not interesting, for it contains random samples from the data set). Although the map is not as clearly defined as the one for garbled English words – the data are clearly much com-

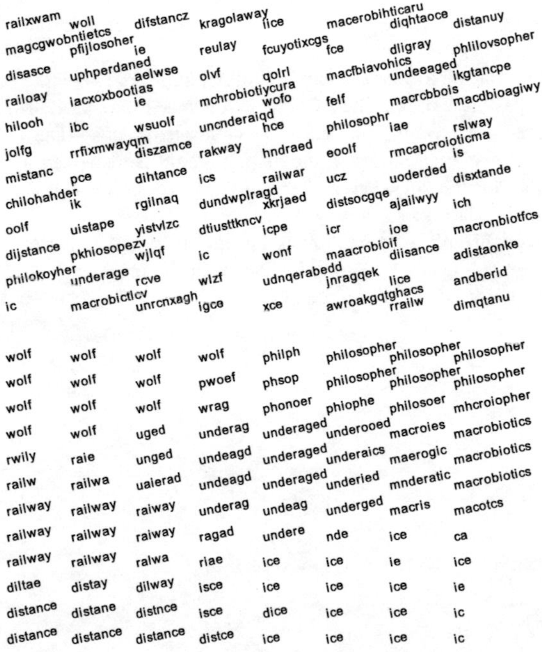

railxwam woll difstancz kragolaway lice macerobihticaru diqhtaoce distanuy
magcgwobntietcs pfijlosoher ie reulay fcuyotixcgs fce dligray phililovsopher
disasce uphperdaned aelwse olvf qolrl macfbiavohics undeeaged ikgtancpe
railoay iacxoxbootias ie mchrobiotiycura wofo felf macrcbbois macdbioagiwy
hilooh ibc wsuolf uncnderaiqd hce philosophr lae rslway
jolfg rrfixmwayqm diszamce rakway hndraed eoolf rmcapcroioticma is
mistanc pce dihtance ics railwar ucz uoderded disxtande
chilohahder ik rgilnaq dundwplragd xkrjaed distsocgqe ajailwyy ich
oolf uistape yistvlzc dtiusttkncv icpe icr ioe macronbiotfcs
dijstance pkhiosopezv wjlqf lc wonf maacrobioif diisance adistaonke
philokoyher underage rcve wlzf udnqerabedd jnraqqek lice andberid
ic macrobicticv unrcnxagh igce xce awroakgqtghacs rrailw dimqtanu

wolf wolf wolf wolf philph philosopher philosopher philosopher
wolf wolf wolf pwoef phsop philosopher philosopher philosopher
wolf wolf wolf wrag phonoer phlophe philosoer mhcroiopher
wolf wolf uged underag underaged underooed macroies macrobiotics
rwily raie unged undeagd underaged underaics maeroglc macrobiotics
railw railwa uaierad undeagd underaged underied mnderatic macrobiotics
railway railway raiway underag undeag underged macris macotcs
railway railway raiway ragad undere nde ice ca
railway railway ralwa riae ice ice ie ice
diltae distay dilway isce ice ice ice ie
distance distane distnce isce dice ice ice ic
distance distance distance distce ice ice ice ic

Figure 3.18: SOM for seven English words corrupted by noise. **Above:** Initial map with corrupted words randomly distributed over it. **Below:** The converged map after 200 iterations. The algorithm has extracted the original (prototypic) words from the noisy set and ordered them into distinct regions on the map. Artificial "transition" words appear on regions borders.

plexer – a few closed areas appear, belonging to distinct classes. Between them, nodes with artificial strings provide for a somewhat smooth transition.

For the much simpler hemoglobine data, the SOM reaches a well defined state already after 1000 iterations, using $\eta = 0.2$ (Figure 3.20). Each class occupies about a half of the map. However, the subclusters, supposed on the Sammon map, do not form recognizably closed ares and are therefore not shown. Using a larger map and a more conservative $\eta = 0.02$, the subclusters emerge, although not very visible (Figure 3.21).

In the SOM for the five kinase families, all families are expressed in the map, but not equally (Figure 3.22). The AGC (map top, black) and CMGC (right edge, light gray) are well recognizable and form compact regions. The PTK family (dotted) occupies a large portion of the map, as could be expected, most visibly left bottom. This is the largest compact family, with over 100 samples in the set. The OPK family (dark gray) is very diverse and thus less expressed. Its traces are weakly recognizable across the map, but it mostly gets taken over by other families. Likewise, the CaMK family (white), which is represented by merely 42 samples in the set, gradually dissolves in the neighboring, larger families.

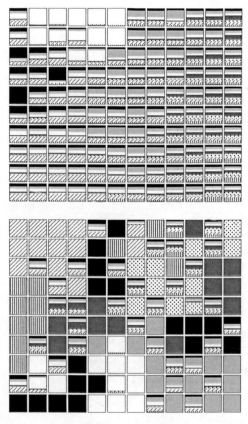

Figure 3.19: SOM for seven protein families. **Above:** At the beginning of the training. Each family is represented by a fill pattern. For a node – represented by a square – the area filled by a pattern corresponds to the similarity of the node to the family. As can be seen, the map is largely undifferentiated. **Below:** The map after 7500 training cycles. Although the set is hard to map onto a two dimensional space (see Figure 3.4), clearly differentiated areas appear in the map. Transitional nodes between them share a similarity with the adjacent areas.

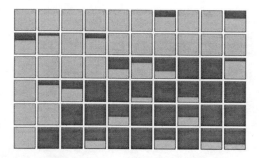

Figure 3.20: SOM for hemoglobine α and β chains. The map is nicely differentiated, with α chain in the lower right area, and β chain above it.

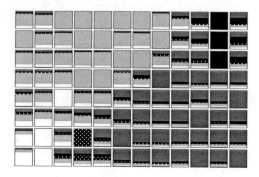

Figure 3.21: A bigger SOM for hemoglobine α and β chains, with visible subclusters. Dark areas symbolize α chain and light areas β chain. α-A is represented by pure black and α-D by white-dotted black. Also, light gray represents the main β chain (mammals) and white others.

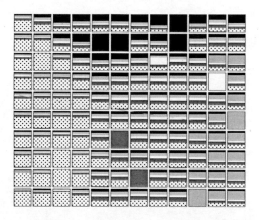

Figure 3.22: SOM for the five kinase families, obtained with 3600 iterations, starting with the neighborhood radius $r = 3$ and $eta = 0.05$. The map represents all five families according to their size and specificity. The largest specific family, PTK (dotted), occupies the largest part of the map. The other, almost as large family, OPK (dark gray) is very diverse and accordingly less expressed. Another less recognizable family, CaMK (white) is relatively small and therefore assigned less space on the map. The remaining two families, ACG (black) and CMGC (light gray) are well expressed.

Chapter 4

Distance-Based Pattern Classification

The purpose of classification algorithms is to find rules for classifying unknown data into a finite number of classes, which are known in advance. By unknown it is meant that the classifier has never encountered the data before, especially not during training. Of course, a trained classifier can also be applied to classify known data, but this task is trivial. Training or learning is the process of extracting the rules by analyzing a data sample for which class memberships are known. Such data can be obtained, for example, by letting an expert manually classify them. The class information attached to the data is commonly called labeling. Since classes are discrete, it has been common to label them by integers, or binary vectors. This is more an implementation convenience than a real need. Classes can be equally well labeled by letters or any other symbols, like "oak", U_{235}, C_2H_5OH or "charm". Any labeling scheme can be translated into another by a simple one-to-one mapping without influencing the meaning.

Like in clustering, distance-based classification methods rely on the assumption that the probability for two data to belong to the same class depends on proximity between them. Classification of unknown data is therefore achieved by observing their distances to landmark points with known labeling. Such points can be seen as representative points in a certain neighborhood, much the same as cluster centers are used to represent clusters. Due to prevailing application to numerical data, such points are usually called reference, model, prototype, or codebook *vectors* in the literature. In this thesis, to include non-vectorial data, I will use more general terms, like reference or model points, or simply references, models, or prototypes.

4.1   Modeling the data

Like in clustering, it is useful to model the data by assuming a process which generates them, and a superimposed noise. The observed points can thus be regarded as samples from some probability distribution $p(x)$. Even better, each class C_j can be modeled by a separate conditional probability $p(x|C_j)$. In the training set each sample is labeled, so it is known which distribution generated it. During recall, when presented an unlabeled datum x, the classifier makes the least error if it assigns the datum to the class with the highest conditional probability at its coordinates, $p(C_j|x)$. This can be found from the class distributions, taking also sizes of classes (their prior probabilities) into account:

$$p(C_j|x) = \frac{p(x|C_j)p(C_j)}{p(x)} \tag{4.1}$$

This is the well-known Bayesian equation. For classification, the denominator, $p(x)$, can be discarded, since it is constant for all classes and influences only the absolute sizes, but not the relationship between different conditional class probabilities. For two classes, C_j and C_k, if $p(C_j|x) > p(C_k|x)$, i.e. if

$$\frac{p(x|C_j)p(C_j)}{p(x)} > \frac{p(x|C_k)p(C_k)}{p(x)} \tag{4.2}$$

then

$$p(x|C_j)p(C_j) > p(x|C_k)p(C_k) \tag{4.3}$$

because $p(x)$ is non-negative by definition.

Figure 4.1 shows hypothetical probability distributions of a two-dimensional data set, unconditional and conditional for two classes. Unfortunately, in real world applications – in contrast to this simple example – the exact forms of the distributions are unknown. We only have observations which form the training set – a finite-size sample. The best we can do is to use them to estimate the probabilities.

Distance-based classification is similar to distance-based clustering, for both use prototypes to model the distribution. There are also some important differences. The basic difference is that in classification, conditional distributions have to be modeled, one for each class. Another detail, making classification easier than clustering, is that for classification the exact data distribution inside classes does not matter. It suffices to model it roughly, so that relationships between distributions for different classes remain preserved. The only criterion for assigning a datum x to a class C_j is that the distribution density $p(C_j|x)$ is higher than any $p(C_k|x)$ for all $k \neq j$. It does not matter *how much* higher it is. Taking again the example from Figure 4.1, it suffices to look at the graph "from above" (Figure

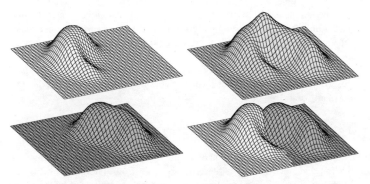

Figure 4.1: Probability density for a two-dimensional sample distribution. **Left:** Conditional probability density for one (**above**) and the other class (**below**). **Right:** Unconditional probability density for the whole data set (**above**) and the higher of the two conditional densities (**below**).

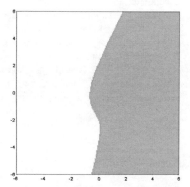

Figure 4.2: A look "from above" at the conditional distribution from Figure 4.1, right below. The class boundary is recognizable without knowing the exact densities.

4.2), just to see which of the classes has the higher density for given coordinates. In this simple example, the class boundary (transition from white to gray) can be described by a single curve. Some pattern classification techniques, most notably those based on scalar product, completely ignore the distribution densities and model the class boundary explicitly. In distance-based methods, the boundary is given implicitly, by estimated class densities.

The probability density at given coordinates is the ratio between the probability to observe a point in the segment S (the neighborhood) around the coordinates and the volume of the segment:

$$p(x) = \lim_{V_S \to 0} \frac{P(x \in S(x))}{V_S} \qquad (4.4)$$

with $S(x)$ denoting the neighborhood of x and V_S its volume. In practical pattern classification tasks, where only a finite number N of observations is available, the probability $P(x \in S(x))$ is unknown and can be approximated by counting the observations in a finite-sized neighborhood around x, say in a hypersphere or hypercube centered at x. If there are k such observations, the density can be approximated by

$$p(x) \approx \frac{k}{NV_S} \qquad (4.5)$$

This approximation leads to the average density in the neighborhood and to the same dilemma already encountered in Chapter 3, when discussing the self-organizing map. Since the number of observations in a neighborhood, usually denoted by k, is an integer, the quotient becomes more accurate with larger k. With only a finite number of observations, the only way to increase k is to increase the volume of the neighborhood. On the other hand, the average better approximates the true density if the neighborhood is chosen small. But, in a neighborhood too small, the danger is that no observations will be found. Such an estimation would lead to the density of zero almost everywhere, except at a finite number of disjunctive areas surrounding the observations, where it would protrude like spikes. Again, there is a trade-off between accuracy and smoothness of the approximation.

4.2 K-Nearest Neighbors

A compromise solution is to make the neighborhood data-dependent. This can be done by choosing a constant K in advance and letting the neighborhood vary in volume until it includes exactly K observations. This way, the neighborhood is chosen wide in areas where observations are sparse and narrow in densely populated areas. If during the recall the distribution remains roughly the same, this

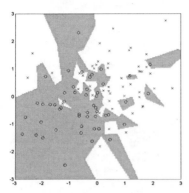 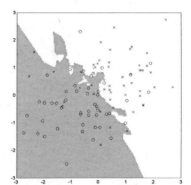

Figure 4.3: Class area estimation by the simple nearest neighbor rule. The classes in this sample overlap significantly and the estimate includes "patches" of one class in wide areas belonging to the other.

Figure 4.4: Class area estimation by the K-nearest neighbor rule, with $K = 7$. The estimated class boundary is smoother and simpler than in the Figure 4.4.

leads to a higher spatial resolution in areas where more unlabeled data are expected, i.e. to a higher precision where it is needed. For classifying an unknown datum x the classifier needs not to estimate the density at all. It suffices to take a neighborhood with K observations from the training set and assign the datum to the most-represented class among them. This "relative majority vote" approach is very simple and intuitive, but at the same time effective. For the reasons of symmetry, the neighborhood is chosen spherical, centered around the unknown datum. The K observations in it are then the K nearest neighbors of the datum, where again any suitable metric can be used.

The basic variant, with $K = 1$, is known simply as the nearest neighbor classification rule. Interestingly, already this rule has very good asymptotic properties. In terms of least expected error, the theoretically best performance a classifier can offer is the one of the Bayesian classifier, which chooses the class with the highest $p(\mathcal{C}_j|x)$. In order to achieve this performance, a classifier would have to be able to know the exact probability distribution. With an infinite training set at disposal, the nearest-neighbor classifier would perform at most twice as bad (Cover and Hart, 1967). In other words, no classifier, no matter how sophisticated, could cut the error of the simple nearest neighbor classifier by more than half. The practical relevance of this statement might seem questionable, for no infinite training set can ever be available. However, this argument applies to all classifiers which rely on a probability density estimation, or some derivative of it.

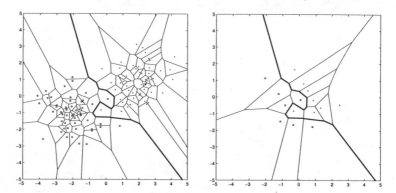

Figure 4.5: Left: Voronoi tesselation of the original data set and the class boundary. Right: Voronoi tesselation of the reduced data set, with only boundary points present. The boundary remains unchanged.

From a practical point of view, the main weakness of the simple nearest neighbor rule is its poor generalization ability, as demonstrated in Figure 4.3. Graphically, one can say that the nearest neighbor rule performs a very patchy estimation of classes. Using a $K > 1$ leads to a kind of smoothing, as displayed in Figure 4.4 and, consequently, better generalization.

"Training" of a nearest neighbor and a K-nearest neighbors classifier is so simple that it hardly deserves the name. It consists simply of storing the training data, together with the associated labels. In the 1960s, when the methods were introduced, memory requirements were an important issue. Storing the whole training set was often impractical or prohibitively expensive. In addition, computational complexity of recall rises with the size of the training set, because for an unknown point, its distances to all stored points have to be computed before making a decision. So the computational effort saved in learning is more than compensated by extra costs during recall.

To counter these problems various methods have been devised for "condensing" (Hart, 1968, Swonger, 1972, Tomek, 1976, Gowda and Krishna, 1979) or "reducing" (Gates, 1974) the data. These algorithms depart even more from the goal of estimating the density and go towards approximating only the class boundary. The basic idea, common to all algorithms is simple: points far behind the class boundary need not be stored, because they are already surrounded by neighbors of the same class. Consequently, an unlabeled point falling in far behind the boundary will be correctly classified, even if some training set points are missing. Following this logic and propagating towards the boundary, one can discard all points from the training set except those nearest to the boundary. A two-dimensional, two classes example with the simple nearest neighbor rule is shown in Figure 4.5.

The first and simplest condensing algorithm Hart (1968) can be described in a couple of lines (Algorithm 4.1).

Algorithm 4.1: Condensed nearest neighbor

1: Set up three sets: the training set $T = \{x_1, x_2, \dots x_N\}$, and two initially empty sets S (store) and G (grabbag).
2: Transfer the first point, x_1, from T to S.
3: **repeat**
4:     Take the next point from T an put it into x.
5:     Classify x by the nearest-neighbor rule, using S as the references.
6:     **if** the classification is correct **then**
7:         Transfer x into G.
8:     **else**
9:         Transfer x into S.
10:     **end if**
11: **until** T is exhausted.
12: **repeat**
13:     Take the next point from G an put it into x.
14:     Classify x by the nearest-neighbor rule, using S as the references.
15:     **if** the classification is wrong **then**
16:         Transfer x into S.
17:     **end if**
18: **until** G is exhausted or there has been one complete pass through G without any transfers taking place.

This is a simple heuristic algorithm, with no established theoretical properties. Its results depend on the enumeration of points and it works correctly only for $K = 1$. There is no guarantee that it will select only the points near a class boundary, so the set of references can be significantly larger than necessary. Also, this approach does not cover the problem of overfitting. Below, I present another, new heuristics, specifically addressing these questions.

4.2.1 Depleted nearest neighbor

To introduce it, consider a data point belonging to a certain class. To classify it correctly (in the nearest-neighbor sense), there must exist a reference point of the same class which is nearer to it than the nearest reference of the opposite class. Now, if more than one reference of the same class satisfies the condition, all but one can safely be removed without influencing the classification of the point.

But, a danger exists that removing a reference could influence the classification of other points from the set. Therefore, the critical references, those whose removal would cause a misclassification of any point, should be retained, whereas others can safely be removed.

Finding the critical reference points involves a property called *score*. It indicates for how many data points the corresponding support vector is the last one before the class boundary. For a data point, being the last reference before the class boundary is defined as being the furthest reference of the same class which is still nearer to it than the nearest reference of the opposite class, and which is also nearer to that opposite class reference than the point itself. Simply put, both references have to lie in approximately the same direction from the point. In other words, in the triangle defined by the data point, the last reference before the boundary, and the nearest reference of the other class, both edges emanating from the last-before-boundary reference are shorter than the edge connecting the data point and the other reference (see Figure 4.6).

To compute the score, one only needs to go through all data points, find the corresponding last reference before the class boundary and increment its score counter. The critical references will have a score greater than zero, and the others can safely be removed.

The same score can be used for improving the generalization capabilities of the classifier. As long as the noise level is noticeably lower than the signal (the laws or rules governing the data distribution), the points that due to the noise fall into the area of the wrong class are infrequent. Therefore, their corresponding critical reference points will have a significantly lower scores than others. Such references should be removed in order to achieve better generalization properties of the classifier.

The learning algorithm starts with the simple nearest neighbor algorithm and simply stores all the training points as reference points. In the next phase, the references are depleted. The score is computed for each of them, and those with the score below some user-defined threshold are removed. A high threshold means that we are willing to accept more training set points to be misclassified. In case of overlapping classes, this increases the generalization ability. The algorithm can be formalized as follows in Algorithm 4.2.

This algorithm is deterministic. For every traing set it produces the same results irrespective of the enumeration order of the points. Other properties, like asymptotic generalization ability are not theoretically established. Nevertheless, as Figure 4.7 shows, it can lead to a significant reduction in the number of references and at the same time better approximation of the class boundary. One motivation for the algorithm was to choose the references near the boundary. Following this path, the idea of modeling the density is clearly abandoned in favor of modeling the boundary. The boundary is implied by the references, which are

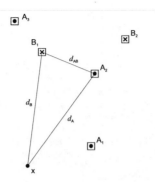

Figure 4.6: Last-before-boundary reference: data point x belongs to the class $\mathcal{A}$. The nearest reference of the class $\mathcal{B}$ is B_1 at the distance d_B from x. The reference A_2, at the distance d_A, is the furthest from x such that $d_A < d_B$ and $d_{AB} < d_B$ and is therefore the last-before-boundary reference for x.

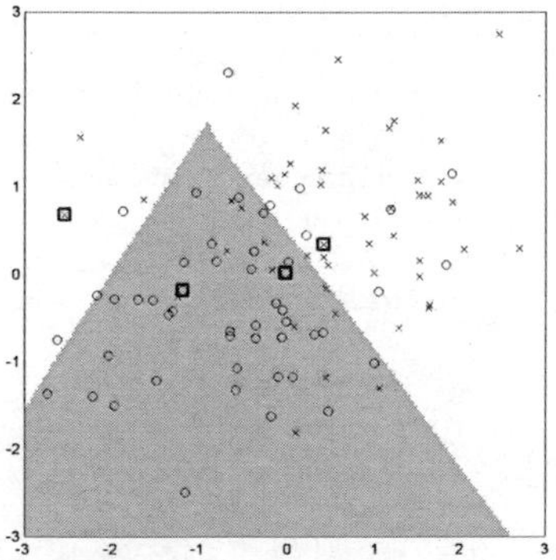

Figure 4.7: Class area estimation by the proposed Depleted nearest neighbor rule, with *Tolerance* = 2. Only the encircled data points have been retained and determine a simple class boundary.

Algorithm 4.2: Depleted nearest neighbor
___
1: Set up two sets: the training set $\mathcal{T} = \{x_1, x_2, \ldots, x_N\}$ and an initially empty set $\mathcal{R}$ (references).
2: Copy all points form from $\mathcal{T}$ to $\mathcal{R}$.
3: **for all** $x \in \mathcal{R}$ **do**
4:    assign a score counter $C(x)$.
5:    Initialize $C(x)$: $C(x) \leftarrow 0$.
6: **end for**
7: **for all** $x \in \mathcal{T}$ **do**
8:    Find its last reference r before the class boundary.
9:    $C(r) \leftarrow C(r) + 1$.
10: **end for**
11: **for all** $x \in \mathcal{R}$ **do**
12:    **if** $C(x) <$ *Tolerance* **then**
13:       Remove x from $\mathcal{R}$
14:    **end if**
15: **end for**

Table 4.1: Classification accuracy of the depleted nearest neighbor algorithm on standard benchmarks, compared to K-nearest neighbors, a multi-layer perceptron, and learning vector quantization. Original tests were divided into a training set ($2/3$ of the original set) and a test set ($1/3$ of the set). The classifiers were trained on the former and the table shows the number of misclassifications of the test data. As can be seen, the performance of the depleted nearest neighbor (dNN) classifier is comparable with other algorithms, but requires significantly less references than K-nearest neighbors. Multi-layer perceptrons (MLP) were trained using Rprop and included one-to-two hidden layers. LVQ was applied with the number of references corresponding to the number of classes.

	Sets size	best K-NN	K	best dNN	Tole-rance	Refe-rences	MLP (range)	LVQ (range)
Cancer	455 + 227	1	7	2	3	4	4 – 15	1
Iris	99 + 51	3	1	3	0	22	5 – 6	6 – 7
Wine	119 + 59	2	1	4	3	11	2 – 7	2

members of the training set. Interestingly, although coming from a completely different mathematical background and motivation, support vector machines (SVMs) share the same property, where support vectors play the role of reference points.

Algorithms for reducing the number of references result in a faster recall and need less memory, but at the price of slower and more complex learning. They shift the computational cost from recall towards the learning phase. They are, so to say, not quite as "lazy" as the original K-nearest neighbors, but still apply the same technique in recall, so cannot be considered completely "eager" either.

Table 4.1 shows a comparison of classification accuracy of depleted nearest neighbor and other classification algorithms on standard numerical benchmarks (Murphy and Aha, 1994). The accuracy is comparable to other algorithms, but the number of references is greatly reduced, compared to K-nearest neighbors, which requires the whole training set to be stored.

4.3 Depleted nearest neighbor for strings

Compared to K-nearest neighbors, depleted nearest neighbor is especially interesting for strings, where computing the distance is expensive. In molecular biology, strings are often several hundreds of symbols long. As briefly mentioned in the Introduction, the current approach to classifying unknown sequences is to find a list of similar, known sequences and sort it by the closeness to the query sequence. The classification itself is usually performed by an expert. Since exact comparison of the query with a large number of sequences can be time-consuming, approximative heuristics, like FASTA or BLAST (Altschul et al., 1990) are commonly applied.

By reducing the number of reference strings, a significant speed-up in recall can be obtained: the recall time is proportional to the number of references. The speed-up comes at the price of a longer training. This trade-off is often acceptable and even desired. In many real-world applications, timely response in recall is desired. The training process is performed only once, before the deployment of the recognizer, and, as long it does not take weeks or months, its duration is not critical. For the examples used in this thesis, the training time ranged from five minutes for the English words to about $2\frac{1}{2}$ hours for the kinase data set.

For the sets with corrupted English words, the depleted nearest neighbor with Levenshtein distance was used. The algorithm leads to a significant reduction of reference points. Instead of storing the full set, as the simple nearest neighbor algorithm would do, it stores only about 28% of the set in case of words corrupted with 50% noise, and about 43% for 75% corrupted words, while still maintaining the perfect classification on the training set (*tolerance* = 0). Increasing the *tolerance* to 2 further reduces the number of references to only about 7% of the training set size, and simultaneously causes some 10% of the data to be misclassified (12.4% for 75%-noisy data). Generalization was tested using a separate data set, with 1750 samples, 250 for each class. The model obtained with *tolerance* = 0 results in 75 false assignments (4.3% of the test set), and the model with *tolerance* = 2 classifies 90 samples (5.1%) incorrectly. Figure 4.8 shows the Sammon mapping of the training set and reference strings.

For biological sets, a metric based on the BLOSUM62 scoring matrix was used. On the hemoglobine data set, using *tolerance* = 0, the algorithm produces 16 references. This is only 5% of the original data set. Perfect classification is preserved even when the *tolerance* is increased to two, but the number of reference sequences drops to 10. This behavior is typical for benign distributions, where the functionality of a reference can be easily taken over by another. For hemoglobine data, the *tolerance* is not a very sensitive parameter. Its influence on generalization has been tested up to the value of five. The original set was divided into three subsets, and the classifier trained on two of them and tested on the third. The procedure has been performed for all permutations of the subsets. In all cases, a perfect classification was obtained.

The Sammon mapping of the data and references is shown in Figure 4.9. Most references appear on the class edges facing the opposite class, as for two-dimensional numerical data. However, one reference in the β-chain is mapped in the middle of the class. This suggests that the mapping cannot fully capture the relationships between the data. The reference is a boundary point but this cannot be successfully represented in two dimensions.

For the five kinase families, the results are more interesting. With the zero tol-

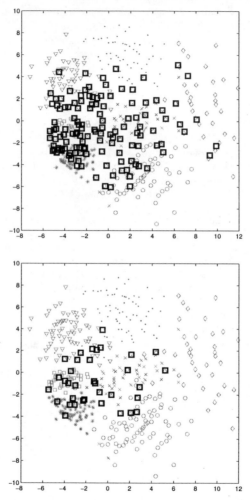

Figure 4.8: Depleted nearest neighbor for the set of seven English words corrupted with 50% noise. The references are highlighted in the original Sammon map of the words. **Above:** References obtained using zero tolerance, allowing for perfect recall. **Below:** With *tolerance* = 2 the number of required references is greatly reduced, at the price of a 10% misclassification of the training data.

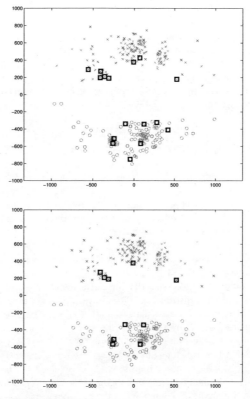

Figure 4.9: Depleted nearest neighbor for hemoglobine data. The figure shows Sammon mapping of the data, α-chain represented as crosses and β-chain as circles. The references are highlighted. **Above:** References obtained using zero tolerance. **Below:** Result obtained with *tolerance* = 2. The perfect classification is preserved with only some 3% of the data set used as references.

erance the algorithm produces a perfect classification of the training set, but needs 51 references. Testing it in the same $2/3 - 1/3$ manner as above shows a few misclassifications — 3, 6 and 7 on different subsets, respectively. This behaviour remains almost unchanged unitl the tolerance of three. Increasing the tolerance to three reduces the number of references to 19, that is less than 5% of the data set. The price we pay is approximately the same number of misclassifications on the training set (18 out of 390), and weaker generalization (7, 9 and 12 misclassifications on the three test subsets). But, looking more closely at the results, it can be seen that mostly the OPK members are misclassified (15 out of total 18 in the whole set and 5, 8 and 10 on the subsets). This can be again explained by the diversity of the OPK class, whose members are often dispersed among other classes. Table 4.2 summarizes the results, and Figure 4.10 represents them graphically.

4.4   Learning Vector Quantization

The K-nearest neighbors algorithm estimates the data density and thus imply the class boundary as a subset of the Voronoi tesselation of the reference points, which actually form the training set. Depleted nearest neighbor and related algorithms reduce the number of needed references but abandon the idea of estimating the class density, and only estimate the boundary.

Learning vector quantization (LVQ) (Kohonen, 1988a,b, 1990, 1995) is a family of classification algorithms which use a limited number of references, but keep them related to class densities. They are somewhat similar to the K-means algorithm, which positions the prototypes (the means) as the centroids of the clusters, as the estimates of density distributions. For classification, not the unconditional data density is relevant, but the class (conditional) densities. Therefore, each class has to be modeled separately by a number of references, or prototypes. Each prototype has roughly the function of the probability that a point falls into its cell under the condition that it belongs to its class. The other Bayesian factor, the unconditional probability of observing the class, is reflected by the number of prototypes assigned to the class: more probable classes are represented by proportionally more prototypes. Having placed the prototypes, the classification of unknown data can be performed by applying the nearest-neighbor rule, now with prototypes serving as neighbors. This mapping of continuous-valued data to a number of discrete values (prototypes) is called quantization, and learning is the process of finding prototype positions in the input space. The algorithms were initially defined on vectorial data, but can be extended beyond them.

LVQ algorithms base on a slight modification and, at the same time, simplification of the above described idea. For classification, only the relationship between class densities is relevant. Unknown data are classified to the class with

Table 4.2: Depleted nearest neighbor for the five kinase families, using *tolerance* = 3. The table shows the number of samples covered by each reference and the number of misclassified samples. Most references, as well as most misclassifications, appear within the OPK class.

		r_1	r_2	r_3	r_4	r_5	r_6	r_7	r_8	r_9	r_{10}
AGC	total		2						19		
	wrong		2								
CMGC	total			1	40			10			30
	wrong			1							
CaMK	total		28			14					
	wrong										
PTK	total	26					24				
	wrong										
OPK	total	1	2	19		6	3			4	2
	wrong	1	2			6	3				2

		r_{11}	r_{12}	r_{13}	r_{14}	r_{15}	r_{16}	r_{17}	r_{18}	r_{19}
AGC	total								50	
	wrong									
CMGC	total									
	wrong									
CaMK	total									
	wrong									
PTK	total					54				
	wrong									
OPK	total	7	5	10	1		2	8	21	1
	wrong									1

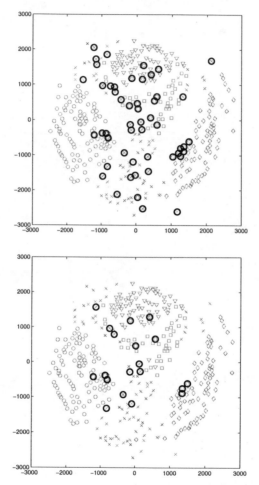

Figure 4.10: Depleted nearest neighbor for the kinase data set. **Above:** using zero tolerance, 51 references (about 13% of the data set) are needed. The references are mapped on
class edges, and most of them are from the OPK class (crosses). **Below:** Increasing the
tolerance to three, the number of references is reduced by almost two thirds. However, 18
samples, mostly from the OPK class, are misclassified.

the highest probability, regardless of how much its probability is higher than of other classes. Therefore, comparing already the two most probable classes suffices. Class boundaries are surfaces where probabilities of the two most probable classes equal. (Theoretically, more than two classes can have the same probability at some point, but, for data from an infinite basic set, the chances are negligible in practice). This suggests not only that modeling the class probabilities is not needed, even modeling the relationship between them all is not needed. It is enough to model the relationship between the two most probable classes in a region.

To model the relationship, let us introduce a function of the two highest class probabilities:

$$\delta(x) = p_T(x) - p_R(x) \tag{4.6}$$

with

$$p_T(x) = p(\mathcal{C}_T|x) \simeq \max_j p(x|\mathcal{C}_j)p(\mathcal{C}_j) \tag{4.7}$$

and

$$p_R(x) = p(\mathcal{C}_R|x) \simeq \max_{j \neq T} p(x|\mathcal{C}_j)p(\mathcal{C}_j) \tag{4.8}$$

(The unconditional probability $p(x)$ has again been left out as irrelevant for classification)

$p_T(x)$ denotes the probability of the most probable ("top" candidate) class, given the datum x, and $p_R(x)$ the probability of the next most probable ("runner-up") class. $\delta(x)$ is always positive except at the class boundary, where it reaches zero. Figure 4.11 shows a simple example with three one-dimensional classes. Of course, with unknown probabilities, $\delta(x)$ is also unknown. LVQ algorithms try to approximate it from observations by positioning the prototypes. In LVQ-terminology, the prototypes are often called "codebook vectors" — a term borrowed from signal processing.

The positioning of prototypes in LVQ algorithms is very similar to the procedure used in self-organizing maps. In both cases, the points from the training set are presented and close prototypes chosen for adaptation. There are also two basic differences. First, in LVQ the prototypes are not topologically organized, so adaptation of a prototype does not include any neighbors. Also, LVQ does not estimate the data density, or directly class probability, but $\delta(x)$, which is the *difference* between two highest class probabilities. Therefore, the adaptation rule differs, depending on whether the prototype belongs to the most probable class or to the second best (runner-up). The former participates positively in $\delta(x)$ and is attracted towards the sampled datum, whereas the latter is repelled, due to its

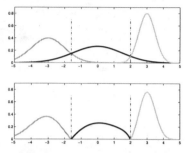

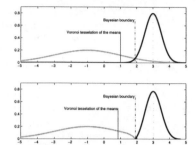

Figure 4.11: Above: 1D-densities of three classes. Below: The differences between the two highest densities. Class boundaries are points where the differences reach zero.

Figure 4.12: Above: 1D-densities of two classes with significantly different dispersions. Below: The differences between the densities. Estimating the class boundary at the mid-point between the two means clearly misses the Bayesian boundary.

negative sign. All other prototypes remain unchanged. This is at least the ideal behavior; different LVQ algorithms make further simplifications.

The simplest and historically the first LVQ algorithm is LVQ1. Its simplification lies in the fact that for each presented datum, the neaerest prototype is always adapted. The adaptation is positive (towards the sample) if the datum and the prototype belong to the same class, otherwise the prototype is repelled. Like in SOM, the amount of attraction and repulsion depends on the distance between the datum and the prototype, and on the ever decreasing learning rate $\eta(t)$. Let $\boldsymbol{\mu}_w$ be the nearest prototype to the training datum $\boldsymbol{x}$, defined exactly as the winner node in SOM (Equation 3.21):

$$w = \arg \min_i d(\boldsymbol{\mu}_i, \boldsymbol{x}) \tag{4.9}$$

The winner is then adapted according to:

$$\boldsymbol{\mu}_w(t+1) = \begin{cases} \boldsymbol{\mu}_w(t) + \eta(t)(\boldsymbol{x} - \boldsymbol{\mu}_w) & \text{for } \boldsymbol{x} \in \mathcal{C}_w \\ \boldsymbol{\mu}_w(t) - \eta(t)(\boldsymbol{x} - \boldsymbol{\mu}_w) & \text{otherwise} \end{cases} \tag{4.10}$$

The complete algorithm is summarized in Algorithm 4.3.

Its performance on a simple artificial data set is shown in Figures 4.13 and 4.14. The above is an on-line algorithm, requires addition and scalar multiplication to be defined and is therefore applicable only for vectorial data. Like for the SOM, a batch version can be formulated. The prototypes tend towards means of "their" their segments of the $\delta(\boldsymbol{x})$ function. Instead of iteratively approaching

---

Algorithm 4.3: On-line LVQ1

1: For each class $\mathcal{C}_j$ put a number of prototypes $\boldsymbol{\mu}_k$ at disposal and initialize them somehow (e.g. randomly).
2: Initialize η to some value $\eta(0)$.
3: **repeat**
4:   Take a random point $\boldsymbol{x}$ from the data set $\mathcal{D}$.
5:   Find the winner prototype $\boldsymbol{\mu}_w : w = \arg\min_i d(\boldsymbol{\mu}_i, \boldsymbol{x})$ (Equation 4.9).
6:   Update $\boldsymbol{\mu}_w$ according to Equation (4.10).
7:   Reduce the learning factor η.
8: **until** the number of iterations reaches some pre-defined limit.

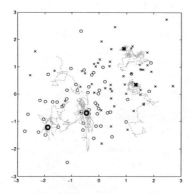 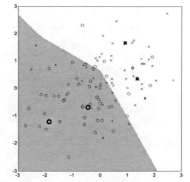

Figure 4.13: Trajectories of four references during training by LVQ1. The positions reached at the end of the training are marked bold.

Figure 4.14: Class areas estimated by four references trained by LVQ1. The class boundary is piece-wise linear and relatively simple.

them, the means can be approximated explicitly from the data. For that purpose
let us define s_{ij} as the sign of the adaptation step:

$$
s_{ij} = \begin{cases} 1 & \text{for } \mu_j \text{ representing the class of } x_i \\ -1 & \text{otherwise} \end{cases} \tag{4.11}
$$

In the simplified, LVQ1 sense, all prototypes from a class different than the class
of x are considered "runner-ups". In that sense, the mean of a δ-function segment
can be expressed as

$$
\mu_j(t+1) = \frac{\sum_{i:x_i \in S} s_{ij} x_i}{\sum_{i:x_i \in S} s_{ij}} \tag{4.12}
$$

S is the segment of the input space represented by $\mu_j(t)$, whose borders and defined by the Voronoi tesselation of the prototypes. The batch LVQ1 algorithm
consists of the steps shown in Algorithm 4.4.

Algorithm 4.4: Batch LVQ1

1: For each class C_j put a number of prototypes μ_k at disposal and initialize them
   somehow (see text).
2: **repeat**
3:    Assign an initially empty set S_j to every prototype μ_j.
4:    **for all** $x_i \in \mathcal{D}$ **do**
5:       Find the winner prototype $\mu_w : w = \arg\min_i d(\mu_i, x)$ (Equation 4.9).
6:       put x_i into S_w.
7:    **end for**
8:    **for all** μ_j **do**
9:       Update μ_j according to (4.12).
10:   **end for**
11: **until** the number of iterations reaches some pre-defined limit.

For initialization, Kohonen recommends ignoring the data labels and using
a SOM for placing the prototypes. Once their initial positions have been determined, each prototype is labeled according to the majority of the data falling in its
segment (Voronoi cell).

Improvements of LVQ1 are known under abbreviations OLVQ1 (optimized-
learning-rate LVQ1), LVQ2, LVQ2.1 and LVQ3. In OLVQ1, the learning rate η
is computed automatically to allow the fastest convergence. In LVQ2, LVQ2.1
and LVQ3 algorithms, two prototypes are always adapted, corresponding to the
top and runner-up. In practice, however, the improved algorithms lead to only
slightly better results. There is also a weakness inherent to all methods which rely
on Voronoi tesselation for determining the class boundary. The estimated class

boundary passes exactly the half-way between cell representatives for different classes. This is acceptable if the distributions in the cells are comparable, but might be quite wrong if class dispersions differ significantly (Figure 4.12). This problem can be countered by using more prototypes than classes.

4.5   Learning Vector Quantization for strings

Like SOM and K-means, LVQ can be defined on strings over a suitable metric and an algorithm for adapting the prototypes. The prototypes can be adapted using a simple modification of the string averaging Algorihtm 2.1. This algorithm only provides for attracting the prototypes towards sample data. LVQ also repels them, if they belong to a different class.

Repelling cannot be directly implemented on strings (there are no "directions" in the string space), but a similar effect can be obtained by using a negative weighting for the symbols, in analogy with the Equation (4.12). Of course, the cumulative weight of symbols must be limited to positive values, otherwise the equation 2.28 makes no sense. This is analogous to batch LVQ for numerical data: Kohonen suggests updating a prototype only if the denominator of (4.12) is positive.

Learning vector quantization was tested on the 50%-noise and the 75%-noise corrupted English words. The tests were performed with seven and 14 prototype strings, two per class. The behavior is similar to K-means: the prototypes converge towards the original words, or close to them. For example, the prototype for the class distance might converge to distnc. The results are visualized in Figure 4.15.

When using 14 prototypes, they obviously could not all converge to the original words. Instead, they tended to divide the classes among themselves, so that each represented a part of it. Two kinds of behavior could be observed: In one, one of the prototypes represented a major part of its class and was close or identical to the original word. The other represented only outliers and beared little resemblence to the original word. The other possibility was to have both prototypes close, but not identical to the original words, like for the classes underaged and ice (Table 4.3). On the separate, 1750-samples test set, in all cases about 200 words (11%–13% of the set) are misclassified. Graphically, the position of the prototypes among the training data is shown in Figures 4.15 – 4.16.

The K-means example has already shown that the hemoglobine family can be prefectly represented by prototypes, based on a distance measure. It is no surprise that LVQ, as a closely related algorithm, achieves a perfect classification of the data. In the experiments, six prototypes were used, because in the Sammon mapping the classes look stretched. But, like for K-means, already two prototypes are sufficient to cover almost the whole set (Table 4.4). All data are correctly classi-

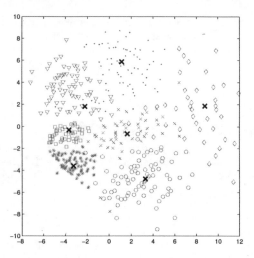

Figure 4.15: Mapping of LVQ for the set of English words corrupted by 50% noise. Seven prototypes – one for each class – were used.

fied even if the other four prototypes are left out. The same behavior is observed when training the classifier on $2/3$ of the data and testing it on the remaining third. In all cases, the perfect classification is obtained, both using 6 and 2 prototypes.

For the five kinase families, the prototypes are distributed among the data (see Figure 4.18), but cover different classes better than the prototypes obtained by K-means. The prototypes were found by training the classifier on different subsets covering $2/3$ of the data and testing the accuracy on the remaining $1/3$. Also, two different learning factors were tested, $\eta = 0.02$ and $\eta = 0.05$, repeatedly in several runs. The prototypes which performed the best on the test set were later used for classifying all data. Using five prototypes, one per class, 7–9 misclassifications (about 2 % of the training set) are obtained. The prototypes were obtained after 3000 iterations and using $\eta = 0.05$. With the same parameters, but using 10 prototypes (two per class), the number of misclassifications could be reduced further to only five or six (about 1.3%), although occasionally up to 11 misclassifications have been obtained. Tables 4.5 and 4.6 summarize the results.

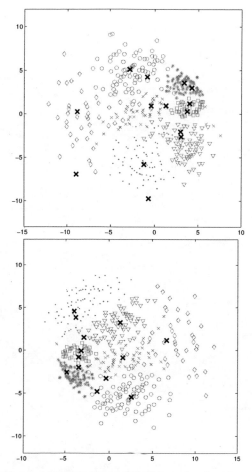

Figure 4.16: Mapping of LVQ for the set of English words, using 14 prototypes. **Above:** Corrupted by 50% noise. **Below:** Corrupted by 75% noise. Two prototypes for each class were used.

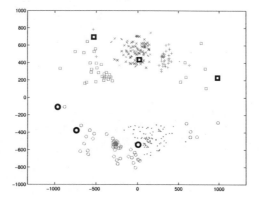

Figure 4.17: LVQ for two hemoglobine chains. Six prototypes, three for each class, are mapped on the original Sammon map of the proteins. The classification is correct for all data but, similarly to K-means, not all six prototypes are needed.

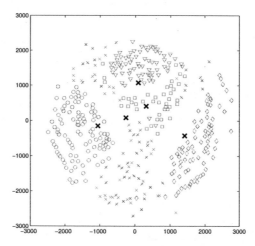

Figure 4.18: LVQ for the kinase data set. Five prototypes, one for each class, are mapped on the original Sammon map of the proteins. The classification is almost perfect.

Table 4.3: Prototypes obtained by LVQ for garbled english words. LVQ with 14 prototypes was applied on 50%-corrupted words. Because there are more prototypes than classes, the prototypes divide the classes in disjoint areas. As a result, they often do not correspond to the original data.

ice	wolf	railway	distance
ie	wolf	railway	distance
ic	ol	raifway	distnc

underaged	philosopher	macrobiotics
underage	philospher	acrobiotics
unhrahed	ghtlabwophkpcekr	awroakgqtghacs

Table 4.4: LVQ classification of hemoglobine α and β chains using six prototypes. α_i and β_i are the prototypes for the two classes, and N_α and N_β denote the number of sequences from each class that are represented by the prototype. All sequences are correctly classified, and, as the table shows, already two prototypes, α_2 and β_2 represent almost the whole set.

	α_1	α_2	α_3	β_1	β_2	β_3
N_α	5	159	1	0	0	0
N_β	0	0	0	2	154	1

Table 4.5: LVQ classification of the five kinase classes, using one prototype per class. The table shows how many sequences are covered by each prototype and how many are misclassified. Compared with the depleted nearest neighbor, the accuracy is much higher, although less references are used. Only eight sequences are misclassified and each prototype clearly represents a family. Interestingly, even the diverse OPK family is well recognized, although still the most likely to be misclassified.

		μ_1	μ_2	μ_3	μ_4	μ_5
AGC	total	69		2		
	wrong			2		
CMGC	total		80			1
	wrong					1
CaMK	total			42		
	wrong					
PTK	total				104	
	wrong					
OPK	total	1	2	1	1	87
	wrong	1	2	1	1	

Table 4.6: LVQ classification of the five kinase classes, using two prototypes per class. The classification accuracy is only slightly improved, compared to the case where only five prototypes were used. Compared to the depleted nearest neighbor, the accuracy is much higher, although less references are used. For the AGC, CaMK and PTK classes, one prototype obviously suffices to cover them almost completely. Also for the CMGC and OPK, one prototype covers the biggest part of the class, and the other covers only 10 samples in each case.

		μ_1	μ_2	μ_3	μ_4	μ_5	μ_6	μ_7	μ_8	μ_9	μ_{10}
AGC	total	69	1			1					
	wrong					1					
CMGC	total			70	10			1			
	wrong								1		
CaMK	total					41	1				
	wrong										
PTK	total							102	2		
	wrong										
OPK	total			2	1					79	10
	wrong			2	1						

Table 4.7: LVQ classification of seven protein family samples, using 15 prototypes, on average two per class. μ_{ij} denotes the j-th prototype of the i-th class and N_i is the number of elements from class i assigned to the prototype in the corresponding column. In this set, 12 sequences are incorrectly classified.

		μ_1	μ_2	μ_3	μ_4	μ_5	μ_6	μ_7	μ_8
N_1	total	3	3	3					
	wrong								
N_2	total				2	8			
	wrong								
N_3	total						6		
	wrong								
N_4	total		1					7	1
	wrong		1						
N_5	total								1
	wrong								1
N_6	total					1			
	wrong					1			
N_7	total					2	1		
	wrong					2	1		

		μ_9	μ_{10}	μ_{11}	μ_{12}	μ_{13}	μ_{14}	μ_{15}
N_1	total							
	wrong							
N_2	total							
	wrong							
N_3	total						2	
	wrong						2	
N_4	total	1						
	wrong	1						
N_5	total	5	2		2			
	wrong				2			
N_6	total	1		4	1	3		
	wrong	1						
N_7	total						3	3
	wrong							

Chapter 5

Kernel-Based Classification

In the previous chapter we saw how a classifier can be trained to approximate class probabilities or their differences. Estimated class boundaries were given implicitly by such approximations. There is, however, an essential problem with approximating class probabilities and data density in general: the number of data needed for a reliable approximation rises exponentially with the data dimensionality. This behavior is known as the *curse of dimensionality*.

It has already been mentioned that for the optimal classification it suffices to know only the class boundaries. It is therefore a tempting idea to approximate them explicitly by some function and so circumvent the density/class probability estimation. This will not completely solve the problems rising from the curse of dimensionality, but can reduce them by a considerable factor. In a D-dimensional input space, the boundary is a $(D-1)$-dimensional hypersurface: curve in a plane, surface in a 3D-space and so on. The density function is more complex, it is a D-dimensional function in a $(D + 1)$ dimensional space: D input dimensions plus one for the density value.

In a general case, depending on class distributions, the boundary can be arbitrarily complex. Modeling it exactly would require a function with arbitrary many parameters – obviously an infeasible approach. But, more than that, overly complex models are not likely to model the boundary more accurately. On the contrary, such models are susceptible to noise, may be mislead by trying to approximate it and can actually lead to a poorer estimation of the boundary. This problem is analogous to the problem of estimating class regions, discussed in the previous chapter. We saw that the simple nearest neighbor classifier is likely to produce a patchy estimation of classes. To counter this risk, we tried reducing the number of prototypes – in other words, simplification of the model – and noted that it leads to better generalization.

To limit the complexity of the boundary model it is common to limit the number of parameters determining it. This can be done in different ways. The most

107

simple is certainly to fix the number of parameters explicitly to some well-chosen value. Somewhat more sophisticated is to make it data-dependent, but include a mechanism to discourage its excessive rise.

One boundary separates two classes. Cases with more classes are easily decomposed into a number of two-class problems. For example, one can consider each class and determine the boundary separating it from all others. For K classes, this leads to K independent boundaries. Another, more costly, but reportedl better possibility is to find the boundary for each pair of classes (Kreßel, 1999). It therefore suffices to discuss only two-class cases.

5.1   Linear class boundaries

The simplest boundary between two classes is the linear function. To be exact, the function is generally an affine one, but the term "linear" is more commonly used. For a vector $\boldsymbol{x} = [x_1, x_2, \ldots, x_D]^{\mathrm{T}}$, such a boundary has the form:

$$
\begin{aligned}
f_a(\boldsymbol{x}) = f_a([x_1, x_2, \ldots, x_D]^{\mathrm{T}}) &= w_1 x_1 + w_2 x_2 + \ldots + w_D x_D + b \\
&= \langle \boldsymbol{w}, \boldsymbol{x} \rangle + b
\end{aligned}
\tag{5.1}
$$

In the context of pattern recognition, the parameters $w_1, w_2, \ldots$ are usually called weights and the parameter b is known as "bias".

The weights, including the bias, are the parameters of the classifier and define the class boundary, the hyperplane separating the classes. The learning process consists of determining their values. Having trained the classifier, the classification of unknown data is simple: one needs only to see at which side of the linear function (hyperplane in a general case) they lie. This is quickly done by calculating their scalar product with the weight vector $\boldsymbol{w}$. On one side of the boundary the product will be positive, and on the other negative. At the boundary itself, the product equals zero. Obviously, this approach can only be pursued if a scalar product is defined.

Various algorithms for determining the optimal linear boundary (under different definitions of optimality) are known (Fisher, 1936, Rosenblatt, 1958, Widrow and Hoff, 1960). They are not essential for this thesis and will not be discussed in depth here. But, as a motivation for support vector machines, which are based on kernels, it is useful to take a brief look at one of them.

Let us use $+1$ and -1 as class labels and denote the label of the vector $\boldsymbol{x}_i$ by t_i (t standing for "target", or desired output of the classifier). Then we can define the error of the classifier as:

$$
E = \sum_i (t_i - \langle \boldsymbol{w}, \boldsymbol{x}_i \rangle)^2
\tag{5.2}
$$

Each vector x_i participates in the error depending on the difference between its target value (label) and actual classifier output. For all vectors from one class, say C_1, the classifier should ideally give $+1$ as the output, and -1 for the class C_2. This ideal can be attained only if a hyperplane exists, such that all $x \in C_1$ lie parallel to it at the distance of 1 at its one side, and all $x \in C_2$ on such hyperplane on its other side. This will normally not be the case, and the error (5.2) will be greater than zero. We can define the optimal classifier (optimal linear separator) as the one minimizing it. In the minimum:

$$\frac{\partial E}{\partial w_j} = 2 \sum_i x_{ij}(t_i - \langle w, x_i \rangle) = 0 \tag{5.3}$$

for every w_j. This leads to a system of linear equations, but, for demonstration purposes, let us take a different approach and assume the system were nonlinear. In that cases, gradient descent methods can help. A training algorithm for linear classifiers which applies this approach is the Widrow-Hoff (Widrow and Hoff, 1960) algorithm, also known as Adaline. The name is an abbreviation for Adaptive Linear Elements, a linear neural network model developed in the 1960s. The algorithm can be expressed as in Algorithm 5.1.

Algorithm 5.1: Widrow-Hoff (Adaline) algorithm (batch version)

1: $w \leftarrow 0$
2: **repeat**
3: $\quad w \leftarrow w + \eta \sum_i x_i(t_i - \langle w, x_i \rangle)$
4: **until** some stopping criterion is met.

In the algorithm, η is the user-defined learning rate parameter, $0 < \eta < 1$. The stopping criterion can be defined as reaching a pre-defined number of iterations, or convergence of w. The term $(t - \langle w, x \rangle)$, the difference between the target and actual output, is sometimes denoted with the Greek letter δ (delta), so the Widrow-Hoff weight adaptation rule is also known as "delta-rule".

For developing kernel-based methods, it is important to note that in w only vectors x_i participate, weighted by corresponding δ_i and η. Consequently, the weight vector can be expressed as the weighted sum of the input vectors:

$$w = \sum_j \alpha_j x_j \tag{5.4}$$

where α_j are some scalar participation weights. Using this representation we can rewrite the update rule (Step 3):

$$\sum_j \alpha_j(n+1)x_j = \sum_j \alpha_j(n)x_j + \eta \sum_i x_i(t_i - \langle \sum_j \alpha_j(n)x_j, x_i \rangle) =$$

$$\sum_j \alpha_j(n)\boldsymbol{x}_j + \eta \sum_i \boldsymbol{x}_i(t_i - \sum_j \alpha_j(n)\langle \boldsymbol{x}_j, \boldsymbol{x}_i \rangle) =$$

$$\sum_j \alpha_j(n)\boldsymbol{x}_j + \eta \sum_j \boldsymbol{x}_j(t_j - \sum_i \alpha_i(n)\langle \boldsymbol{x}_i, \boldsymbol{x}_j \rangle) =$$

$$\sum_j \boldsymbol{x}_j \left[\alpha_j(n) + \eta(t_j - \sum_i \alpha_i(i)\langle \boldsymbol{x}_i, \boldsymbol{x}_j \rangle) \right] \qquad (5.5)$$

and, consequently:

$$\alpha_j(n+1) = \alpha_j(n) + \eta \left(t_j - \sum_i \alpha_i(n)\langle \boldsymbol{x}_i, \boldsymbol{x}_j \rangle \right) \qquad (5.6)$$

All scalars α_j can be put together into a vector $\boldsymbol{\alpha}$. The whole Adaline algorithm can be rewritten in an alternative, dual form:

Algorithm 5.2: Widrow-Hoff (Adaline) algorithm (dual form)

1: $\boldsymbol{\alpha} \leftarrow \boldsymbol{0}$
2: **repeat**
3:    **for all** j **do**
4:       $\alpha_j \leftarrow \alpha_j + \eta \left(t_j - \sum_i \alpha_i \langle \boldsymbol{x}_i, \boldsymbol{x}_j \rangle \right)$
5:    **end for**
6: **until** some stopping criterion is met.

It is important to note that in the algorithm, input vectors never appear alone, but only in pairs, in scalar products. The resulting vector $\boldsymbol{w}$, which defines the boundary, is a weighted sum of input vectors, but we do not need to know it explicitly. We saw above that for classifying an unknown datum $\boldsymbol{x}$, it suffices to observe its scalar product with $\boldsymbol{w}$, which can be written as:

$$\langle \boldsymbol{x}, \boldsymbol{w} \rangle = \sum_j \langle \boldsymbol{x}, \alpha_j \boldsymbol{x}_j \rangle \qquad (5.7)$$

As it appears, all we need both for determining the boundary and classification is to have a scalar product defined on the data. This is not only the case for the Adaline algorithm, many other algorithms can be expressed only through scalar products. Together with the notion of a kernel, this will lead us to support vector machines.

5.2   Kernel-induced feature spaces

Linear boundaries are very simple to handle, but also often too constrained for practical purposes. Linearly separable data sets are extremely rare in practice.

Already the simple example in Figure 4.1 shows classes which are not perfectly linearly separable. A satisfactory approximation might be possible, depending on how high a misclassification rate are we willing to accept. For more complex cases, a linear approximation would depart even further from the actual class boundary. Obviously, more flexible ways of describing boundaries are needed.

An obvious idea is to choose a more powerful function, like a quadratic or cubic one, and try to use it for approximating the boundary. There is, of course, no guarantee that the chosen function is suitable for the data set, it can only be hoped so. So a general classification algorithm should preferably have a number of functions to choose from. There are also practical problems following from this idea. First, the number of possible functions, or parameters controling them, rises with their order. Also, even if we would provide the classifier with all imaginable functions, it will most probably have to be equipped with a separate learning algorithm for each of them.

The problem of finding a better boundary can be addressed from the other side, too. Instead of looking for a nonlinear discriminant function in the original, input space, one can transform the data in some nonlinear fashion and try to separate them linearly. The effect is the same as using a non-linear function, just that this time we can use known linear learning algorithms. Transforming data is actually a very natural approach and has been used from the very beginnings of pattern recognition research. Scaling is a typical linear transformation applied at the early stages of the pattern recognition process. Feature extraction, which is also used in data preparation, often involves nonlinear transformations, but for different reasons. For example, principal component analysis can be used for dimensionality reduction. The components of transformed vectors are usually called *features*. Appropriately chosen, they actually represent the information inherent in the data. The space of transformed vectors is consequently called *feature space*. Sometimes, the problem can be simplified without reducing the dimensionality, by applying a nonlinear transformation. But, this approach is only applicable if we know in advance which transformation is suitable for the data.

Interestingly, in many cases the problem can be simplified by *increasing* the dimensionality. In a sense, the trick is to exploit the curse of dimensionality for a good purpose. Figure 5.1 shows an example of one-dimensional data where classes are not linearly separable. In one dimension, the linear function is simply a constant, and there exists no constant such that elements of one class are to the left of it and of the other to its right. Transforming the data into a two-dimensional feature space by a simple nonlinear mapping $\phi(x) : x \mapsto [x, x^2]^\top$ renders the classes linearly separable. Of course, this is an artificially constructed educational example (a counterexample is also easy to find), but the principle can be generalized. To get the idea, consider three points in a two-dimensional space, i.e. plane, not lying on a same line. No matter how we label the points, there

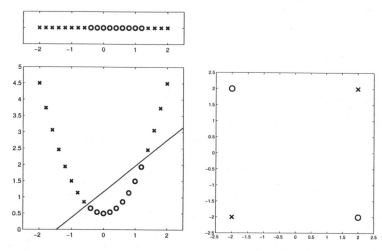

Figure 5.1: Above: Two one-dimensional classes, linearly non-separable. **Below:** by a non-linear transformation into the two-dimensional space, the data become linearly separable.

Figure 5.2: A simple example of two linearly non-separable classes. No line can separate crosses from circles.

is always a line separating one class from the other. But, four points can be labeled in an unsuitable manner, as shown in Figure 5.2. No single line is capable of separating one class from the other. If the points were not lying in a plane, but in a three-dimensional space, there would exist a plane separating the classes. Generally, in a D-dimensional space, $D + 1$ linearly independent points can be arbitrarily separated in two classes, regardless of the labeling. It can be said that a D-dimensional linear classifier has the capacity to perfectly classify any two-class data set of $D + 1$ D-dimensional points. The capacity of a classifier is known as its VC dimension, a term coined by Vladimir Vapnik and Alexei Chervonenkis. Nonlinear classifiers have generally a higher VC dimension.

Increasing the dimensionality by an explicit transformation $\phi(x)$ and using the linear classifier is a well known technique known as generalized linear functions. They have been fairly successful in many tasks, provided a suitable mapping has been chosen. However, using high-dimensional feature space implies high computational complexity, both in space, for storing high-dimensional data, as well as time, for performing the computations over all feature dimensions. Another big family of pattern recognition architectures, neural networks with nonlinear activation functions, perform not only nonlinear transformations, but also imply nonlinear boundary functions. As a consequence, they are more powerful than generalized linear classifiers in the same feature space, but are susceptible to local optimums. Since the discriminant function is not linear, gradient descent methods are not guaranteed any more to lead to the globally best parameter settings for describing the boundary.

An explicit transformation enables us to represent each datum in the feature space. As we have seen in the Adaline example above, explicit knowledge of each datum is not necessary for finding the class boundary. In its dual form, the Adaline algorithm was formulated to work only with scalar products, never needing single data. Consequently, to find the boundary in the feature space, we only need to know scalar products there. The scalar product, $\langle \phi(x), \phi(y) \rangle$ can be seen as a bivariate scalar function $K(x, y)$, for it takes two vectors as arguments and returns a scalar:

$$K(x, y) = \langle \phi(x), \phi(y) \rangle \tag{5.8}$$

Such a function is called a *kernel*, the name coming from integral operator theory, which forms a theoretical basis for describing relationships between kernels and feature spaces. With an appropriate choice of the mapping $\phi(x)$, the feature-space scalar product $K(x, y)$ can be easy to compute, easier than the transformation itself. For example, consider the mapping from a two-dimensional input space onto a three-dimensional feature space:

$$\phi(x) = \phi([x_1, x_2]^\mathsf{T}) = [x_1^2, x_2^2, \sqrt{2}x_1x_2]^\mathsf{T} \tag{5.9}$$

It is easy to see that the scalar product $\langle \phi(x), \phi(y) \rangle$ can be written as:

$$\langle \phi(x), \phi(y) \rangle = \langle x, y \rangle^2 \tag{5.10}$$

In other words, the kernel is computed at a marginally higher cost than the scalar product in the input space, simply by squaring it.

In this example, we constructed the kernel explicitly from a known nonlinear mapping. But for the linear classifier it does not matter, it works without knowing the mapping. So the problem of choosing an appropriate transformation can be reformulated as the problem of finding a suitable kernel. The mapping itself is irrelevant and, interestingly, we are able to formulate kernels without even knowing how the associated mapping looks like. It can be said that a kernel induces a feature space.

It is clear that not every scalar function of two variables is a kernel. Being essentially scalar products, they have to satisfy some conditions. Mathematically general conditions for compact subsets $X \subseteq \mathbf{R}^D$ and all functions $f \in L_2(X)$ are given by Mercer's theorem and require that

$$\int_{X \times X} K(x, y) f(x) f(y) dx dx \geq 0 \tag{5.11}$$

where $K(x, y)$ is a continuous symmetric function (see e.g. Cristianini and Shawe-Taylor, 2000, p. 35). In practice, having only a finite number of observations, this condition can be expressed as a condition on the matrix K of all kernel values, $K = [k_{ij}]_{i,j=1}^{N} = [K(x_i, x_j)]_{i,j=1}^{N}$. This matrix is called the *kernel matrix* and Mercer's theorem implies that that it must be positive semi-definite. A kernel matrix is actually a Gram matrix in the feature space, and a Gram matrix is always positive semi-definite.

Among the most popular kernels for vectorial data are polynomial kernels:

$$K(x, y) = \langle x, y \rangle^d \tag{5.12}$$

and

$$K(x, y) = (\langle x, y \rangle + c)^d, \tag{5.13}$$

as well as the Gaussian kernel

$$K(x, y) = \exp\left(-\frac{\|x - y\|^2}{2\sigma^2}\right) \tag{5.14}$$

The VC-dimensionality of polynomial kernels depends on the data dimensionality and on the user-defined parameter d. The Gaussian kernel has an infinite VC-dimensionality, it can separate arbitrarily many points in any desired way. For it, the highest kernel value is one and is reached for two identical points; kernel value of any two different points is less than one. This somewhat resembles the nearest neighbor classifier, where the proximity is the highest for two identical points and falls with the distance between them.

In practice, even non-kernels have been used with promising results. One such "kernel" is the sigmoid function:

$$K(x, y) = \tanh(\langle x, y \rangle + \theta) \tag{5.15}$$

Extension to non-vectorial data is straightforward. Since the classifier needs only kernel values, it is irrelevant of which type the original data are. It suffices that a kernel is defined on them. In Section 5.4 we shall see how kernels can be defined on strings.

5.3 Support Vector Machines

With a kernel defined, we can apply any linear learning algorithm for estimating the class boundary, provided the algorithm can be expressed in the dual form, using only scalar computation and scalar products. However, different algorithms estimate different boundaries and not all can be equally suitable. Is there a rule for choosing the algorithm, or can one algorithm be generally preferred?

Statistical learning theory, developed by Vladimir Vapnik and Alexei Chervonenkis, addresses these questions from the generalization point of view. For a fixed training set of N points and a classifier (called "hypothesis class" in VC-terminology) with a certain capacity (VC-dimension) d, it is shown that the best generalization is achieved when the classifier makes the minimum number N_E of misclassifications of the training data, as intuitively expected. With a probability $1 - \delta$ the generalization error satisfies:

$$\varepsilon_{\text{gen}} \leq \frac{2N_E}{N} + \frac{4}{N}\left(d\log\frac{2eN}{d} + \log\frac{4}{\delta}\right) \tag{5.16}$$

provided the samples forming the training set are drawn independently and in an identical way, and $d \leq N$ (see Cristianini and Shawe-Taylor, 2000).

The number of misclassifications is an empirical value, thus the approach is called *empirical risk minimization*. However, if we increase the classifier's VC-dimension, the impact on the generalization error can vary. On one hand, more complex classifiers will make less errors on the training set: N_E and the first term above will fall. On the other hand, overly complex classifiers can produce too complex boundaries, perhaps perfectly classifying the training set, but being poor in generalization. This behavior is reflected in the rise of the second term in the equation above.

Let us suppose having a sequence of nested hypothesis classes, such that a more complex class always includes all simpler ones. The optimal classifier can be chosen by starting with the simplest, which makes many misclassifications on the training set, and gradually increasing its capacity until the rise in the second term outweighs the decrease in the first term, i.e. until the bound on the generalization error starts to rise. This approach is known as *structural risk minimization*.

The practical inconvenience with it lies in forming the nested set of hypothesis classes. But the fundamental problem is that it explicitly relies on the VC-dimension of the classifier. According to the Equation (5.16), classifiers with a high VC-dimension (e.g. infinite, like Gaussian kernel) would not be capable of learning at all, no matter how trivial the data distribution. Intuitively, this is hard to believe. Equation (5.16), giving a universal – that is, worst case – bound, includes no reference to the distribution. Is it possible to make the bound tighter, at least for "benign" distributions, by providing some information about them?

A crucial result from statistical learning theory is that the generalization ability can be expressed in terms of a property called *margin* and independently of the VC-dimension. In case of a linear classifier, we are looking for the best separating hyperplane. For a hyperplane defined by the vector w and bias b, the margin of a training set example (x_i, t_i) is simply the value:

$$\gamma_i = t_i(\langle w, x_i \rangle + b) \tag{5.17}$$

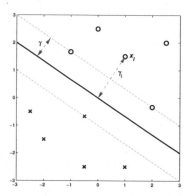

Figure 5.3: Margins: γ_i denotes the margin of the point x_i and γ the data set margin.

This type of margin is called *functional*, for it is the value of the linear function, multiplied by the class label. This value is not unique for a fixed hyperplane and the point, because the same hyperplane can be defined in an infinite number of ways, simply by scaling w and b by some factor. It is therefore more useful to rely on the *geometric* margin, which is the functional margin with w normalized to the length of one:

$$\gamma_i = \frac{t_i}{\|w\|}(\langle w, x_i \rangle + b) \tag{5.18}$$

The margin of a hyperplane over the whole training set is the minimum margin over all points from the set. The other way round, the margin of a training set is the maximum margin over all hyperplanes. The hyperplane with the maximum margin is the *maximal margin hyperplane*. In the case of linearly separable classes, the margin is always positive (Figure 5.3).

According to statistical learning theory, the generalization error of a linear classifier is minimized by maximizing its margin. Since the norm of w appears in the denominator, this is equal to minimizing $\langle w, w \rangle$. But, this approach can be pursued only if the margin is positive and sufficiently large with respect to the training set size – a condition which is satisfied only for linearly separable data with relatively little noise. For such data, the problem of finding the best separating hyperplane can be expressed as constrained optimization problem. The minimization of the squared norm $\langle w, w \rangle$ has to be done while satisfying the conditions for all data being on the correct side of the margin:

$$\text{minimize} \quad \langle w, w \rangle$$
$$\text{subject to:} \quad t_i \left(\langle w, x_i \rangle + b \right) \geq 1 \tag{5.19}$$

The minimization is equal to minimizing the Lagrangian:

$$L(\boldsymbol{w}, b, \boldsymbol{\alpha}) = \frac{1}{2}\langle \boldsymbol{w}, \boldsymbol{w} \rangle - \sum_{i=1}^{N} \alpha_i \left[t_i \left(\langle \boldsymbol{w}_i, \boldsymbol{x}_i \rangle + b \right) - 1 \right] \tag{5.20}$$

By differentiating it with respect to $\boldsymbol{w}$ and b and substituting the obtained relations in the above equation, the dual form is obtained ((Cristianini and Shawe-Taylor, 2000)):

$$L(\boldsymbol{w}, b, \boldsymbol{\alpha}) = \sum_{i=1}^{N} \alpha_i - \frac{1}{2} \sum_{i=1}^{N} \sum_{j=1}^{N} \alpha_i \alpha_j t_i t_j \langle \boldsymbol{x}_i, \boldsymbol{x}_j \rangle \tag{5.21}$$

Thus the optimal weight vector $\boldsymbol{w}^* = \sum_i t_i \alpha_i \boldsymbol{x}_i$ of the separating hyperplane is obtained by solving the following problem:

$$\text{maximize} \quad \sum_{i=1}^{N} \alpha_i - \frac{1}{2} \sum_{i=1}^{N} \sum_{j=1}^{N} \alpha_i \alpha_j t_i t_j \langle \boldsymbol{x}_i, \boldsymbol{x}_j \rangle \tag{5.22}$$

$$\text{subject to:} \quad \sum_{i=1}^{N} \alpha_i t_i = 0$$

$$\alpha_i \geq 0$$

The offset b does not appear here and has to be found by relying on the primal representation:

$$b^* = -\frac{\max_{t_i=-1}\langle \boldsymbol{w}^*, \boldsymbol{x}_i \rangle + \min_{t_i=1}\langle \boldsymbol{w}^*, \boldsymbol{x}_i \rangle}{2} \tag{5.23}$$

The problem of finding the optimal $\boldsymbol{w}^*$ is a quadratic optimization problem with linear constraints. Such problems are called convex quadratic programmes and the optimization theory has developed powerful machinery for solving them. It would be beyond the scope of this thesis to get into depths of the theory or to describe specific algorithms. Let it just be stated that minimizing a function $f(\boldsymbol{w})$, $f \in C^1$ on a convex domain $\Omega \subseteq \mathbf{R}^n$, subject to affine constraints $g(\boldsymbol{w}) \leq 0$ and $h(\boldsymbol{w}) = 0$ can be done using the generalized Lagrangian:

$$L(\boldsymbol{w}, \boldsymbol{\alpha}, \boldsymbol{\beta}) = f(\boldsymbol{w}) + +\boldsymbol{\alpha}^\mathsf{T} g(\boldsymbol{w}) + \boldsymbol{\beta}^\mathsf{T} h(\boldsymbol{w}) \tag{5.24}$$

The point $\boldsymbol{w}^*$ is an optimum iff there exist $\boldsymbol{\alpha}^*$, $\boldsymbol{\beta}^*$ such that:

$$\frac{\partial L(\boldsymbol{w}^*, \boldsymbol{\alpha}^*, \boldsymbol{\beta}^*)}{\partial \boldsymbol{w}} = 0$$

$$\frac{\partial L(\boldsymbol{w}^*, \boldsymbol{\alpha}^*, \boldsymbol{\beta}^*)}{\partial \boldsymbol{\beta}} = 0$$

$$\boldsymbol{\alpha}^{*\mathsf{T}} y(\boldsymbol{w}^*) = 0 \tag{5.25}$$

$$g(\boldsymbol{w}^*) \leq 0$$

$$\boldsymbol{\alpha}^* \geq 0$$

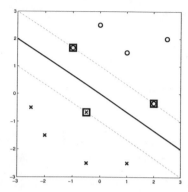

Figure 5.4: Support vectors of a sample data set (squares) determine the maximal margin linear function separating the classes.

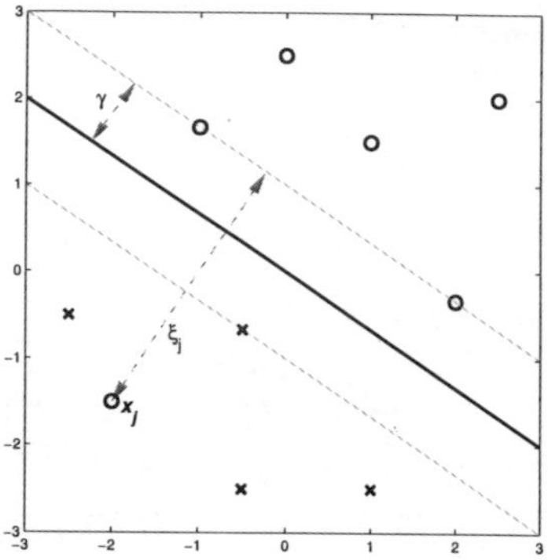

Figure 5.5: The point x_j (circle) lies deeply inside the other class (crosses). The slack variable ξ_j is its distance from "its" side of the margin.

The third relation above is known as the Karush-Kuhn-Tucker complementary condition. A big advantage of quadratic programmes is that they have only one optimum, so there is no danger of getting stuck in a local optimum – a problem plaguing neural networks.

For the problem stated in Equation (5.23) it is interesting to observe the structure of the solution. From the Karush-Kuhn-Tucker complementary condition it follows that:

$$\alpha_i^* \left[t_i \left(\langle w^*, x_i \rangle + b^* \right) - 1 \right] = 0 \tag{5.26}$$

which essentially means that the optimum lies either inside the convex area, so the constraints represented by α are inactive, or on an area edge or vertex, with corresponding constraints α_i active.

The result in (5.26) is zero when either α_i^* or the term in the square brackets is zero. The term in the brackets is zero only for the input points with the margin of one, so their corresponding α_i^* is nonzero. For all other points, which have the margin greater than one and are further away from the hyperplane, their α_i^* must be zero. Hence only the points on the one-margin participate in describing the weight vector w^* and all other can be discarded. The margin points can be seen as supporting the hyperplane and are called *support vectors* (Figure 5.4). The quadratic optimization problem above was given for the input-space variables x_i. By noting that the points never appear alone but only inside scalar products, extending the algorithm to kernel-induced feature spaces is straightforward. One only needs to substitute inner products with kernels and the task becomes:

$$\text{maximize} \quad \sum_{i=1}^{N} \alpha_i - \frac{1}{2} \sum_{i=1}^{N} \sum_{j=1}^{N} \alpha_i \alpha_j t_i t_j K(\boldsymbol{x}_i, \boldsymbol{x}_j)$$

$$\text{subject to:} \quad \sum_{i=1}^{N} \alpha_i t_i = 0$$

$$\alpha_i \geq 0 \tag{5.27}$$

with

$$b^* = -\frac{\max_{t_i=-1} K(\boldsymbol{w}^*, \boldsymbol{x}_i) + \min_{t_i=1} K(\boldsymbol{w}^*, \boldsymbol{x}_i)}{2} \tag{5.28}$$

where

$$K(\boldsymbol{w}^*, \boldsymbol{x}_i) = \sum_{j=1}^{N} \alpha_j^* K(\boldsymbol{x}_i, \boldsymbol{x}_j) \tag{5.29}$$

If, as normally the case, the classes are not linearly separable or the margin is small, the above *maximal margin classifier* cannot be used. Its objective is hard: all training points must lie "outside" the margin, i.e. have the margin at least equal to one. For non-separable classes this is impossible, for there exist points with a negative margin. For such cases, the *soft margin* approach is to allow points inside the margin or even on the wrong side of the separating hyperplane, but to include a punishment term, discouraging such points.

Allowing the margin to be violated is easily done by introducing a slack variable ξ_i for every point (Figure 5.5). The optimization constraint is thus changed from:

$$t_i \left(\langle \boldsymbol{w}, \boldsymbol{x}_i \rangle + b \right) \geq 1 \tag{5.30}$$

to

$$t_i \left(\langle \boldsymbol{w}, \boldsymbol{x}_i \rangle + b \right) \geq 1 - \xi_i, \quad \xi_i \geq 0 \tag{5.31}$$

and the punishment term is a norm of the vector $\boldsymbol{\xi}$, multiplied by the user-specified constant C. The punishment term is included into the objective function. Using the l_1 norm, the optimization task in the primal form becomes:

$$\text{minimize} \quad \langle \boldsymbol{w}, \boldsymbol{w} \rangle + C \sum_{i=1}^{N} \xi_i$$

$$\text{subject to:} \quad t_i \left(\langle \boldsymbol{w}, \boldsymbol{x}_i \rangle + b \right) \geq 1 - \xi_i \tag{5.32}$$

$$\xi_i \geq 0$$

Represented in the dual form and for kernel-induced feature space, the task is to

$$\text{maximize} \quad \sum_{i=1}^{N} \alpha_i - \frac{1}{2} \sum_{i=1}^{N} \sum_{j=1}^{N} \alpha_i \alpha_j t_i t_j K(\boldsymbol{x}_i, \boldsymbol{x}_j)$$

$$\text{subject to:} \quad \sum_{i=1}^{N} \alpha_i t_i = 0$$

$$C \geq \alpha_i \geq 0 \tag{5.33}$$

In other words, the l_1-soft margin approach differs from the maximal margin approach only by constraining the Lagrange multipliers from above by C.

Another possibility is to use the l_2 (Euclidean) norm of $\boldsymbol{\xi}$ as the punishment term. The optimization problem then becomes:

$$\text{maximize} \quad \sum_{i=1}^{N} \alpha_i - \frac{1}{2} \sum_{i=1}^{N} \sum_{j=1}^{N} \alpha_i \alpha_j t_i t_j \left(K(\boldsymbol{x}_i, \boldsymbol{x}_j) + \frac{\delta_{ij}}{C} \right)$$

$$\text{subject to:} \quad \sum_{i=1}^{N} \alpha_i t_i = 0$$

$$\alpha_i \geq 0 \tag{5.34}$$

where δ_{ij} is the Kronecker delta: $\delta_{ij} = 1$ for $i = j$ and 0 otherwise. The difference between l_2-soft margin and maximal margin lies only in adding the $1/C$ to the diagonal elements of the kernel matrix.

As we see, all three kinds of support vector machines can be trained by solving essentially the same kind of problem. Compared to the basic, maximal margin SVM, the other two differ only slightly in constraints or in the effectively used kernel matrix.

Figures 5.6–5.9 show the performance of the l_1-soft margin SVM on the sample set already used in Chapter 4. In all cases, the Lagrange factors were limited from above by $C = 100$. As one can see, the machines produce a large number of support vectors (points in squares), which is due to the considerable overlap of the classes.

5.4   String kernels

Support vector machines can be applied to string data by defining a kernel function for strings. At the time of the writing of this thesis, extensive research on this topic is performed, often in connection with molecular biology or speech recognition. An early kernel for strings is described by Watkins (1999), and a number of others have been proposed, e.g. (Lodhi et al., 2000, Leslie et al., 2002, Vert,

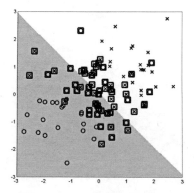

Figure 5.6: Support vector machine was applied to the sample data set in the input space, i.e. using scalar product of the data and not a kernel. Due to the simple structure of the data (two overlapping Gaussian classes) the boundary determined by the SVM matches the Bayesian quite well.

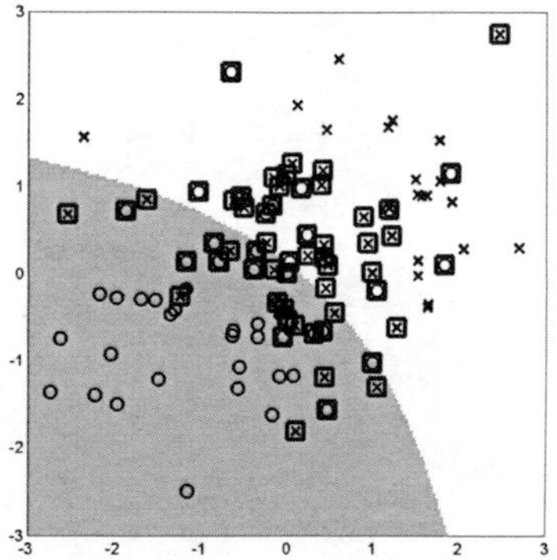

Figure 5.7: Classes as predicted by a SVM with a quadratic kernel $K(x,y) = (2 + \langle x, y \rangle)^2$. The class boundary resembles a smoothed version of the boundary in Figures 4.7 and 4.14.

2002, Shimodaira et al., 2002, Campbell, 2002). Due to the ongoing research, no final review can be given here. Instead, the kernel by Watkins is briefly presented, as a motivation for two yet unpublished kernels.

The Watkins kernel relies on two facts. First, a joint probability distribution is a valid kernel if it is conditionally symmetrically independent (CSI), that is, if it is a mixture of a countable number of symmetric independent distributions:

$$
\begin{aligned}
p(x, y) &= p(y, x) = \sum_{c \in \mathcal{C}} p(x|c)p(y|c)p(c) = \\
&= \sum_{c \in \mathcal{C}} \left[p(x|c)\sqrt{p(c)} \right] \left[p(y|c)\sqrt{p(c)} \right] = \\
&= \phi(x) \cdot \phi(y) = K(x, y)
\end{aligned}
\tag{5.35}
$$

where $\mathcal{C}$ is the set of possible values of the random variable c, on which x and y are conditioned.

Second, two strings a and b can be considered random variables, generated by a pair hidden Markov model (PHMM). A PHMM is a Markov model which emits two sequences, not necessarily of the same length. Its states can be divided into four groups:

1. S^{AB}: States that emit two symbols, one for the sequence A and one for B,

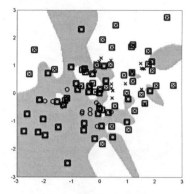

Figure 5.8: Result of a SVM with a Gaussian kernel, $\sigma = 0.25$. The class estimates are patchy, resembling the nearest neighbor classifier (Figure 4.3).

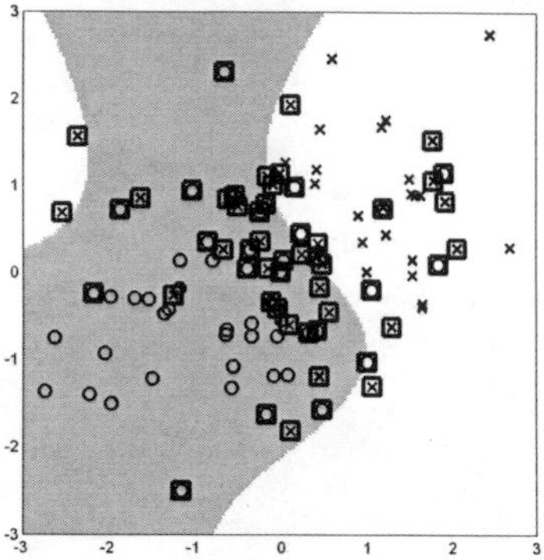

Figure 5.9: Result of a SVM with a Gaussian kernel, $\sigma = 1.5$. The class boundary is considerably simpler than in Figure 5.8.

2. S^A: States that emit only the symbol for the sequence A.

3. S^B: States that emit only the symbol for the sequence B.

4. S^-: States that emit no symbols.

The states in the fourth group are only for notational convenience and do not play a part in the output. If the PHMM is conditionally symmetrically independent, the probability that it will simultaneously produce the sequences a and b, conditioned on a known sequence c of states from the first group (emitting two symbols), can be written as

$$p(a, b|c) = p(a|c)p(b|c) \qquad (5.36)$$

The unconditional probability $p(a, b)$, obtained by summing the conditionals over all possible state sequences c (Equation (5.35)) is hence a valid kernel. On the other hand, $p(a, b)$ can be computed by dynamic programming, similarly to string distance or similarity score. The difference is that the dynamic programming algorithms from the previous section rely on the addition of edit costs at each position, while the probability has to be computed by multiplication of transition probabilities. This is only a detail, and scoring schemes relying on the CSI pair HMM can be used as kernels.

For BLOSUM scoring matrices, which are probably the most popular scoring matrices currently used in comparing amino-acid sequences, it is not established if they can be translated into a CSI PHMM. It would be nevertheless desirable to use them, because they are optimized to reflect the biological properties of proteins. By a simple modification, which retains all the relationships between the amino-acids, a kernel based on the scoring matrices can be defined.

Recall that a scoring matrix is simply a symmetric matrix of similarities for all possible pairs of symbols. Similarly, a kernel matrix is a matrix of kernel values for all pairs of data. A scoring matrix is usually not positive semi-definite, but, like any other matrix, it can be made so by adding a constant term to every element. Using such a modified scoring matrix, the similarity scores will be different than when using the original matrix. But, the *relationship* – the difference – between the scores of different sequence pairs will not change. So the information from the original matrix remains preserved, but the modified matrix can be seen as the kernel matrix of all pairs of amino-acids (the symbols). Two facts are obvious: First, the matrix of similarities for any subset of the symbols is also a kernel matrix. And second, the matrix of similarities for any collection of symbols, even containing repeated symbols, is a kernel matrix. The repeated symbols only lead to zero eigenvalues, leaving the matrix positive semi-definite.

To see that the similarity matrix for a set of sequences is also a kernel matrix, recall that the similarity score of two sequences is simply the sum of similarities of the aligned symbols. To accommodate indels, spaces are considered valid symbols. The similarity matrix for sequences is consequently the sum of the similarity matrices for single symbols, each matrix corresponding to a position in the aligned sequences. From the definition of positive semi-definiteness ($x^{\mathsf{T}}Ax \geq 0$ for all x) it follows directly that the sum of positive semi-definite matrices is also positive semi-definite: $x^{\mathsf{T}}(A + B)x = x^{\mathsf{T}}Ax + x^{\mathsf{T}}Bx \geq 0$. Thus the similarity matrix for a set of sequences is a kernel matrix. It is implicitly understood here that all the aligned sequences have the same length. This can be achieved by padding the shorter ones with spaces, as has been done in multiple alignment, without changing the similarity scores.

The kernel defined over the modified similarity matrix is also a radial kernel, like the Gaussian one. The maximal value is obtained for identical strings. But, contrary to the Gaussian kernel, there is no parameter like the kernel width σ for controlling its smoothness. As a consequence, for data sets where diversity inside classes is high – in other words, where kernel values for identical strings differ much from the values for different ones, – many support vectors may be needed for correct classification. To see this, consider a simple example:

Given are three strings, s_1, s_2, and s_3, together with the corresponding kernel values k_{ij}, $i, j \in \{1, 2, 3\}$. s_1 and s_3 belong to one class (+1), and s_2 to the other (-1). Suppose s_1 and s_2 being support vectors (actually support strings) with the corresponding Lagrangian coefficients α_1 and α_2. Support vectors have the functional margin of one:

$$\alpha_1 k_{11} + \alpha_2 k_{12} = +1$$
$$\alpha_1 k_{12} + \alpha_2 k_{22} = -1.$$

For this kernel, the kernel values are always positive. Also, $k_{ii} \geq k_{ij}$ for all i, j. To correctly classify s_3,

$$\alpha_1 k_{13} + \alpha_2 k_{23} \geq +1$$

must hold. Combining the three formulae, the condition can be expressed as

$$\alpha_1 (k_{11} + k_{12} + k_{13}) + \alpha_2 (k_{22} + k_{12} + k_{23}) \geq +1.$$

Now, if the strings differ significantly, kernel values for identical strings will be much larger than for different ones, so in the sums, k_{ij} can be considered negligible for every $i \neq j$. The above condition can be approximated by

$$\alpha_1 k_{11} + \alpha_2 k_{22} \geq +1.$$

where no reference to s_3 is made. The condition is constant for the given SVM –always satisfied or always violated – and all non-support strings are assigned to the same class. To achieve the correct classification for strings of different classes, they will have to be declared support vectors.

Without the kernel width σ, the same problem would plague the Gaussian kernel. Indeed, when σ is sufficiently small, the SVM behaves like a nearest-neighbor classifier. By choosing an appropriate σ, too different kernel values for identical and different points can be avoided.

In the experiments of Jaakkola and Haussler (1998) a Gaussian function was applied to differences between Fisher scores for proteins. The Fisher scores were obtained from the hidden Markov model trained specifically for the investigated protein family. The HMM probability score actually measures the similarity of the sequence with the model, and the Fisher score for a single sequence s is

$$U(s) = \frac{\partial \log p(s|H(\theta))}{\partial \theta}. \tag{5.37}$$

A kernel can be obtained by applying a Gaussian:

$$K(s_1, s_2) = \exp\left(-\frac{\|U(s_1) - U(s_2)\|^2}{2\sigma^2}\right). \tag{5.38}$$

This gives rise to the idea of relying on a general scoring matrix instead of a specifically trained HMM, and applying the Gaussian on the distance between the strings. PAM scoring matrices imply a hidden Markov model, although not for a protein family, but for all proteins. BLOSUM is an improvement, taking only biologically relevant mutations – those in conserved areas – into account for computing the transition probabilities. Thus a kernel can be defined as

$$K(s_1, s_2) = \exp\left(-\frac{d(s_1 - s_2)^2}{2\sigma^2}\right). \tag{5.39}$$

relying on distance functions described in Section 2.3. This is again a radial kernel, but more flexible than the above one, which relies only on the similarity score.

5.5 Support Vector Machines for strings

For the set of seven corrupted English words, the Gaussian (metric) kernel based on the Levenshtein distance was used. The set could not be perfectly classified, even with $C = 10^6$, which is a very large value, taking into account that most Lagrange coefficients α were smaller than one. By limiting them to $C = 10$, a multi-class SVM (actually a set of 21 two-class SVMs) was obtained with almost perfect classification. In the experiment with $\sigma = 10$, support vectors reached the upper bound in only one two-class SVM, the one separating the class wolf from ice. This is not very surprising, because the support vectors hardly resembled the original words: fl, gc, or lf. The observed behavior was almost the same for the sets with 50% and 75% noise, the latter only produced more support vectors at the upper bound, as could be expected. Similarly, using a different σ did not change the performance very much and only varied the number of support vectors at the upper bound. For $\sigma = 15$ and the data set with 75% noise, two additional pairs of classes could not be perfectly separated and led to support vectors' Lagrange coefficient reaching the upper bound: railway and underaged, and distance and ice. But also in this case, the support vectors themselves were so corrupted with noise that this behavior could be expected. However, the number of support vectors varied largely for different parameters and class pairs, ranging from 14 (approximately 10% of the data) to as many as 112 (2/3 of the data).

Increasing C to 15 had also a positive impact on the generalization abilities of the SVM. Tested on the separate 1750-samples data set, the SVM trained with $C = 10$ had 90 misclassifications on the set with 50% noise, compared to only 41 (2.3% of the set) obtained using $C = 15$. For the set with 75% noise, the respective numbers are 335 and 173.

The two hemoglobine chains can be sucessfully classified using support vector machines with string kernels. Both the simple BLOSUM62 similarity kernel and the Gaussian kernel based on the BLOSUM62-derived distance measure have been tested. The results do not differ much: the Gaussian kernel produces 22 support vectors, and the similarity kernel 25. When using the similarity kernel, only the punishment term C has to be chosen, but the SVM performed equally well using a variety of C's, from 0.2 to 5. For the Gaussian kernel, also the kernel width

σ has to be chosen. The choice of this parameter is somewhat more important, but still not critical. As in the previous chapter, the optimal value was found by trying out different values on a $2/3$ subset of the data and testing the recall on the remaining $1/3$. An initial clue about reasonable σ can be won by observing distances between strings in the set. For the hemoglobine data set, the distances range from several hundred to something over thousand, so corresponding values of σ were tested. The best results were obtained for $\sigma^2 = 5 \cdot 10^5$.

With these parameters, the classes are linearly separable in the kernel space, and the classification is correct for the whole set. As can be deduced from the mapping of the vectors (Figure 5.10), isolated sequences and the sequences on the edges of areas with high data concentration are the preferred choice for support vectors.

For the kinase data set, both Gaussian and similarity kernel reach similar accuracy and generalization ability. But, measured in the number of support vectors, the results using Gaussian are more practical, since they include fewer support vectors. For strings, where kernels are computationally expensive, this might be an issue. For example, for separating the AGC class from CaMK, the SVM with the similarity kernel needs 73 support vectors — out of 113 which comprise the two classes. Using the Gaussian kernel, the same SVM contains only 29 support vectors. The whole multi-class support vector machine is implemented as a set of two-class SVMs, one for each pair of classes.

On this data set, the performance is not very sensitive to parameters, neither for similarity nor for Gaussian kernel. Since the distances in the data set range up to 3000, the Gaussian kernel width was tested in range $\sigma^2 \in [2.5 \cdot 10^6, 1.25 \cdot 10^7]$. For both kernels, the punishment term C was tested in range $[0.2, 8]$, plus infinity. Except for $C < 0.5$, the SVM trained on a $2/3$ of the data set usually had between one and three misclassifications on the remaining $1/3$, although the error never fell to zero. Training the SVM with the same parameters, but on the whole data set, a perfect classification can be achieved.

Trained using the BLOSUM62 similarity kernel, it requires 798 support vectors – almost twice as many as there are sequences in the data set. This is partially due to the fact that the two-class SVMs, comprising the multi-class SVM, are independent, so a sequence can easily be a support vector in more than one two-class SVM.

Using a metric kernel based on the BLOSUM62 scoring matrix and $\sigma^2 = 9 \cdot 10^6$, a perfect classification is obtained with less sequences used as support vectors. The whole SVM requires 409 support vectors, what is still more than the number of sequences in the data set, but about half as many as the SVM with the similarity kernel. As shown in Figure 5.11, some sequences never act as support vectors, whereas others play the role in more than one two-class SVM.

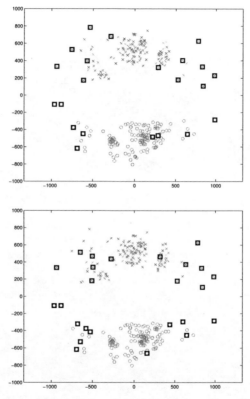

Figure 5.10: Sammon mapping of two hemoglobine chains, with support vectors highlighted. **Above:** Support vectors obtained using the metric kernel. **Below:** Support vectors obtained by the BLOSUM62 similarity kernel. The classification is perfect in both cases. The similarity kernel produces slightly more support vectors than the metric one. Due to the radiality of the kernels, isolated sequences are more likely to become support vectors.

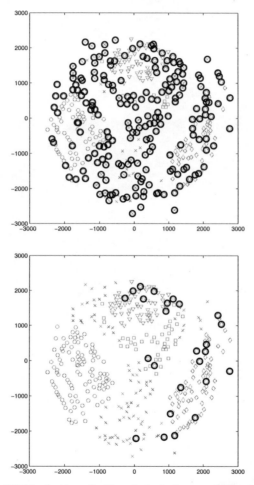

Figure 5.11: SVM for the kinase families, obtained using a metric kernel. **Above:** Sammon mapping of the data set with all support vectors highlighted. **Below:** Only the support vectors of the AGC-CMGC two-class SVM are highlighted. The two classes are well separated, so 25 support vectors suffice: 11 from the AGC class and 14 from the CMGC.

Chapter 6

Spectral Clustering

Support vector machines have been highly successful in pattern classification. Kernel-implied data transformation in a high dimensional space is extremely efficient and the linear boundary in the feature space easily found. Encouraged by their performance in classification, researchers have tried to develop kernel-based methods for clustering.

Already in his Ph.D. thesis, Schölkopf (1997) noted that principal components in the feature space induced by Gaussian kernels reflect input-space areas of higher data density. In (Schölkopf et al., 1999), a so-called one-class classification was introduced. This method provided for finding support vectors which determine areas of high data density. It was not clustering in the common sense, for it gave no information how to divide data into clusters. The same idea, not limited to kernel spaces, was pursued by Tax (2001).

A kernel-based clustering method was proposed by Ben-Hur et al. (2001), but it was not purely feature-space based. It considered the data to form a single cluster in the infinite feature space induced by the Gaussian kernel and determined the support vectors delimiting it. Back in the input space, the paths between support vectors were examined. If the density along the path – that is, kernel values of path points and support vectors – was above some threshold, the path was considered to be inside a cluster. Otherwise, the lowest-density point was taken as the cluster boundary. This approach requires continuity in the input space and is not applicable on discrete data, like strings.

To cluster data completely in feature space, Girolami (2002) adapted the expectation-maximization method of Buhmann (1999), which is in a sense an extension of the K-means algorithm. The adaptation to feature space consisted in expressing the algorithm in terms of scalar products and substituting them with kernel values. However, the algorithm was still a stochastic one and prone to local optimums. Another method, proposed by Cristianini et al. (2002), preformed clustering by analyzing only the kernel matrix or, more exactly, its spectrum. Other spectral clustering methods, not necessarily relying on kernels, have also been intensively examined (Weiss, 1999, Meilă and Shi, 2001, Shi and Malik, 2000, Ng et al., 2002). They all share the common idea of analyzing the eigenvectors and eigenvalues of the affinity matrix in order to discover clusters. Although similar, the algorithms differ in important details. The authors generally agree that spectral clustering methods are still incompletely understood.

In this chapter a clustering algorithm (Fischer and Poland, 2003) is presented which is in some steps similar to the one of Ng et al.. It exploits the fact that cluster membership is reflected in eigenvectors associated with large eigenvalues. The algorithm is capable of producing a hierarchical cluster structure if the data form nested clusters and is therefore more flexible than simple partitioning algorithms. Conditions under which it performs well and under which it is likely to fail are examined, and the behavior illustrated on simple examples. Also, a novel method for computing the affinity matrix is proposed, based on the concept of path conductivity. In it, not only the direct paths between points are considered, but also all indirect links, leading to an overall measure of connectivity between the points. The performance of the algorithms is tested on some hard artificial data sets and on standard benchmarks.

6.1   Clustering and the affinity matrix

The affinity matrix is a weighted adjacency matrix of the data. In a graph-theoretical sense, all data are connected to form a weighted graph, larger weights implying higher similarity between the points. We consider here only non-negative and symmetrical weight functions, resulting in non-negative and symmetrical affinity matrices.

For illustrative purposes, however, we shall start with idealized, unweighted adjacency matrices. The entry $A[i,j]$ at some position (i,j) in the matrix A is set to one if the similarity between two points x_i and x_j is above some fixed threshold. Otherwise, it is set to zero. Since we discuss symmetrical similarity functions, the entry $A[j,i]$ is assigned the same value. Let us now imagine that the data form clear, disjunct clusters C_j, so that the similarity between points belonging to the same cluster is always above the threshold, and below it for points from different clusters. So for all n_1 points belonging to the first cluster there will be n_1^2 1-entries in the matrix, n_2^2 for the n_2 points from the second cluster, and so forth. By appropriately enumerating the points — first all from the first cluster, then from the second etc. — the affinity matrix becomes a block-diagonal matrix, with blocks of sizes $n_1 \times n_1$, $n_2 \times n_2$ and so on.

From the definition of eigenvalues and eigenvectors ($Ae = \lambda e$) it is easy to see that $\lambda_j = n_j$ are the nonzero eigenvalues of A and that the associated eigenvectors e_j can be composed as follows:

$$e_j(i) = \begin{cases} 1 & \text{for all } i : \sum_{k=1}^{j-1} n_k < i \leq \sum_{k=1}^{j} n_k \\ 0 & \text{otherwise} \end{cases} \tag{6.1}$$

The eigenvectors can, of course, be scaled by an arbitrary nonzero factor.

Recalling how the affinity matrix was constructed, it is obvious that the following holds:

$$x_i \in C_j \Leftrightarrow e_j(i) \neq 0 \tag{6.2}$$

This gives us hope that we can cluster data by examining the spectrum of the affinity matrix. Note that the above statement remains true even if we enumerate the points differently, so that A is not block-diagonal. By different enumeration we achieve a permutation of rows and columns of A. However, such a permutation does not change the matrix' eigenvalues, and results only in permuted eigenvectors. Bearing this in mind, we can restrict the discussion to nicely permuted matrices. All results still remain valid, provided they do not depend on the order of entries in the eigenvectors.

Departing from the above simple case, we now allow different weights of graph edges. For numerical data, a convenient weighting function is the Gaussian kernel

$$A[i,j] = \exp\left(-\frac{\|x_i - x_j\|^2}{2\sigma^2}\right) \tag{6.3}$$

As noted by Perona and Freeman (1998), there is nothing magical with this function. Any symmetrical, non-negative function monotonously falling with increasing distance can be applied. A slight advantage of the Gaussian function is that it results in a positive definite affinity matrix – a kernel matrix, – somewhat simplifying the analysis of eigenvalues. The value of kernel width σ has to be provided by the user. The choice of a correct width is critical for the performance of the algorithm. We shall return later to the question how to choose a good σ and assume for the moment that it has a sensible value. Then the points belonging to the same cluster will result in affinity matrix entries close to one, whereas for the points from different clusters, the entries will be close to zero. Thus the matrix still resembles a block-diagonal matrix. Examples illustrating this are given in Figures 6.1 and 6.2. For nicely enumerated data, this suffices for clustering them: we only need to visually inspect the affinity matrix and assign points to a same cluster if their indices belong to the same block. Unfortunately, real-world data are usually wildly permuted, so we need to proceed with spectral analysis.

Using eigenvalue decomposition, an affinity matrix A can be represented as:

$$A = E\Lambda E^\mathsf{T} = \sum_i \lambda_i e_i e_i^\mathsf{T} = \sum_i \lambda_i A_i \tag{6.4}$$

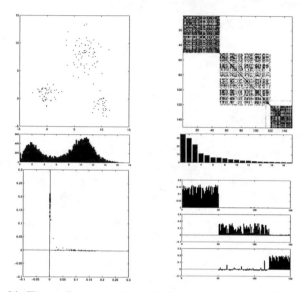

Figure 6.1: Three well separated clusters. **Left column:** scatter plot of the data (top); distance histogram (middle); spectral plot along the 2nd and 3rd eigenvector (bottom). **Right column:** Affinity matrix A of the data (top); 20 largest eigenvalues of A (middle); components of the first three eigenvectors of A (bottom).

Here, the columns of the matrix E are the eigenvectors e_i of A and Λ is a diagonal matrix containing corresponding eigenvalues λ_i. For all eigenvectors $\|e_i\| = 1$ holds. The products $e_i e_i^{\mathsf{T}}$, shortly denoted by A_i, are the rank-1 components. Thus a symmetric matrix can be represented as the sum of its rank-1 components, weighted by the associated eigenvalues.

Contrary to the initial, idealized case with the affinity matrix being strictly block-diagonal, now many (in case of positive definite functions like the Gaussian: all) eigenvalues will be nonzero. The same holds for eigenvector components, rendering our simple algorithm based on the rule (6.2) inapplicable. We shall, however, still rely on it as a motivation. First we note that as the real-valued affinity matrix approaches binary, few clearly dominant eigenvalues emerge. Also, eigenvector components diminish for non-cluster points and approach some clearly defined nonzero value for points belonging to the cluster associated with the eigenvector. To cluster data we can therefore observe the eigenvectors associated with the dominant eigenvalues.

To illustrate the idea, let us observe a block-diagonal-like affinity matrix, like

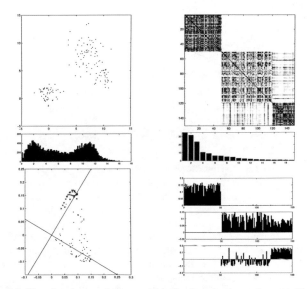

Figure 6.2: Three less separated clusters. Visualized are the same values as in Figure 6.1. The rightmost, lower cluster from Figure 6.1 is shifted upwards towards the central one. Note how a weaker superblock in the affinity matrix appears, encompassing the lower two blocks, and how the spectral plot is rotated.

the one in Figure 6.1, top right. It contains three blocks of different sizes. As can be seen in the same figure, in the graph below the matrix, its first three eigenvalues are larger than the rest, which smoothly fall towards zero. This is an indication that the first three rank-1 components contribute more significantly than others to the affinity matrix. If we take a look at the associated eigenvectors, we see that each of them clearly corresponds to a block. This is not surprising: eigenvector components with large magnitude (either positive or negative) result in large positive values when multiplied with components of the same sign and a comparable magnitude, leading to large entries in the rank-1 component. Small-magnitude entries result in small entries in the component, thus bearing little contribution to the affinity matrix entries. Finally, large positive components multiplied with large negative ones result in large negative entries in the component.

This last case is particularly interesting. Recall that we consider only nonnegative affinity matrices. Thus, negative entries in one rank-1 component must be compensated by positive ones in one or more others (we assume a kernel weighting function, resulting in all nonnegative eigenvalues). For the sake of simplicity, let us suppose that the positive entry at the position (i, j) in the component A_p compensates the negative entry in A_q, either by being larger in magnitude or by belonging to a larger eigenvalue:

$$A_p[i,j] > 0, \qquad A_q[i,j] < 0$$
$$\lambda_p A_p[i,j] > \lambda_p A_p[i,j] + \lambda_q A_q[i,j] > 0 > \lambda_q A_q[i,j] \qquad (6.5)$$

In order to achieve this, the signs of the eigenvector components must obey:

$$\mathrm{sgn}(e_p[i]) = \mathrm{sgn}(e_p[j]), \qquad \mathrm{sgn}(e_q[i]) = -\mathrm{sgn}(e_q[j]) \qquad (6.6)$$

with the consequence that the diagonal entries $A_p[i,i], A_q[i,i], A_p[j,j], A_q[j,j]$ are all positive. In other words, the entries (i, i) and (j, j) get amplified in the affinity matrix, and (i, j) and (j, i) attenuated. What does all this tell us? From the affinity matrix as a whole, we see that the i-th and j-th point share some small degree of similarity. The rank-1 component A_p suggests that they are highly similar, and A_q, with its negative entries, the contrary.

The interpretation we propose is the following: Points x_i and x_j belong to the same cluster, as A_p suggests. At the same time, they belong to two different subclusters, which is reflected in the entries of A_q. We will use this observation later for exploring the hierarchical data structure.

An example illustrating this explanation is shown in Figure 6.2. The data set consists of three clusters, the same ones as in Figure 6.1, but the small rightmost cluster is shifted upwards towards the big central one, so that they partially overlap. The points are nicely enumerated: first all points from the first, then from the second, and finally from the third cluster. In the affinity matrix, two blocks are visible, with the larger containing two smaller subblocks. This structure is reflected in the dominant eigenvectors: the second has large, positive components for all points from the supercluster, whereas the third splits it into two subclusters by positive and negative components.

This example also shows that we have to be cautious with interpretation of eigenvectors. Assigning a point to a cluster if the component of the corresponding eigenvector is above some threshold is a temptingly simple approach, but can easily fail if clusters overlap. Another case when this approach can fail is when space spanned by the dominant eigenvectors is rotation invariant, as is the case when there are more identical eigenvalues. For example, consider the identity matrix as an affinity matrix:

$$\begin{pmatrix} 1 & 0 \\ 0 & 1 \end{pmatrix} \qquad (6.7)$$

An obvious decomposition is $\lambda_1 = 1$, $e_1 = (1, 0)^\mathsf{T}$ and $\lambda_2 = 1$, $e_2 = (0, 1)^\mathsf{T}$. However, an equally valid decomposition is $\lambda_1 = 1$, $e_1 = (1/\sqrt{2}, 1/\sqrt{2})^\mathsf{T}$ and

$\lambda_2 = 1$, $e_2 = (1/\sqrt{2}, -1/\sqrt{2})^{\mathsf{T}}$. In the first case, we would assign the first point to the first and the second to the second cluster. In the second case, the simple approach fails, because the eigenvectors give contradictory information. Not only that the simple approach *can* fail, it *will* fail if we substitute zeros in the matrix with some small nonzero entries, even of the order of 10^{-12}. Then, the matrix will cease to be rotation invariant and the eigenvectors will necessarily be rotated for almost 45 degrees from the axes.

Nevertheless, data clustering by analyzing dominant eigenvectors of the affinity matrix is possible if we take a more sophisticated approach. We begin by noting that for each point x_i only the i-th components of the eigenvectors determine its cluster membership. It has to be so, otherwise a different enumeration of points would influence the clustering. So we form a set of K-dimensional vectors y_i, whose components are the i-th components of the K dominant eigenvectors:

$$
\begin{aligned}
y_i(1) &= e_1(i) \\
y_i(2) &= e_2(i) \\
&\vdots \\
y_i(K) &= e_K(i)
\end{aligned}
\tag{6.8}
$$

For points from the same cluster, the corresponding y-vectors are in a sense similar. If we draw them as points in a K-dimensional spectral space, we see that the similarity is of a specific kind. For clearly distinct, convex clusters, the points in the spectral graph are nicely distributed along straight lines passing through the origin (Figure 6.1). As clusters begin to overlap, the points disperse angularly around the lines. The lines, in addition, get rotated proportional to the degree the clusters form a common supercluster (Figure 6.2). Thus the problem of clustering original points x_i can be transformed into clustering their spectral images y_i. The latter problem is easier to solve, due to the line-like distribution of the images: we only need to find the typical vector, the one lying on the line, for each cluster.

6.2 Algorithm overview

The proposed clustering algorithm consists only of a couple of steps (Algorithm 6.1): The first two steps are straightforward, the third needs some elaboration, and the last three form the core of our clustering algorithm.

We noted earlier that the Gaussian kernel is a common function for building the affinity matrix of numerical data. Its key parameter is the kernel width σ and the algorithm performance heavily depends on it. In our work, we determine it from the distance histogram. In a common sense, a cluster is a set of points sharing some higher level of proximity. So if the data form clusters, the histogram of

---

Algorithm 6.1: Spectral clustering

1: Build the affinity matrix.

2: Compute the eigenvalues and eigenvectors of the matrix.

3: Discover dominant eigenvalues.

4: Analyze the eigenvectors associated with the dominant eigenvalues and find typical values for their components.

5: Build the clusters according to eigenvector components' similarity to typical values.

6: Analyze relationship of typical eigenvalue components to discover hierarchical data structure.

---

their distances is multi-modal, the first mode corresponding to the average intra-cluster distance and others to between-cluster distances. By choosing σ around the first mode, the affinity values of points forming a cluster can be expected to be significantly larger than others. Consequently, the affinity matrix resembles a block-diagonal matrix or its permutation. Once the matrix has been built, computing eigenvalues and eigenvectors is easy. We do not even need to compute all n eigenvalues, we just need the largest. How many, depends on the number of clusters, but it will certainly be at least an order of magnitude smaller than the number of points. Reducing the number of eigenvalues significantly speeds up the algorithm.

Our algorithm analyzes the eigenvectors bearing the most clustering information. We have reasoned above that these are the vectors associated with the dominant eigenvalues. So once eigenvalues are known, we have to find how many of them are dominant. For data sets forming clearly separated, convex and not too elongated clusters, there is a significant drop between dominant and non-dominant values (see Figure 6.1). For more complex data sets, the choice can be harder, because the eigenvalues decrease smoothly. A method proposed by Girolami (2002) relies on dominant terms in

$$\sum_{i=1}^{N} \lambda_i \{\mathbf{1}_n{}^{\mathsf{T}} e_i\}^2 \tag{6.9}$$

where $\mathbf{1}_n$ is a shorthand notation for an n-dimensional vector with all components equal to $1/n$, n being the number of points. It was claimed that if there are K distinct clusters within the data, there are K dominant terms $\lambda_i \{\mathbf{1}_n{}^{\mathsf{T}} e_i\}^2$ in the above summation. The statement was illustrated by several examples, but counterexamples are also easy to find. Consider the identity matrix (6.7) from the previous section: depending on the eigenvalue decomposition we choose, we obtain either two dominant terms, both equal to one, or only one term equal to two. Generally it can be said that the method is likely to fail when clusters overlap, but is worth trying if no obvious dominant eigenvalues exist.

Once we have decided on the number of eigenvectors to use, we form a set of spectral images y_i of the original data x_i by transposing the eigenvectors, as described by Equation (6.8). To cluster them, we employ an algorithm we term "K-lines". It is a modification of K-means and relies on point distances from lines instead of from means (Algorithm 6.2).

Algorithm 6.2: K-lines clustering

1: Initialize vectors $m_1...m_K$ (e.g. randomly, or as the first K eigenvectors of the spectral data y_i).
2: **repeat**
3:    **for** $i \leftarrow 1 ... K$ **do**
4:       Define $\mathcal{P}_j$ as the set of indices of all points y_i that are closest to the line defined by m_j.
5:       Create the matrix M_j : $M_j \leftarrow [y_i]_{i \in \mathcal{P}_i}$ whose columns are the corresponding vectors y_i
6:    **end for**
7: **until** m_j's do not change

The mean vectors m_j are prototype vectors for each cluster scaled to the unit length. Each m_j defines a line through the origin. By computing m_j as principal eigenvector of $M_j M_j{}^\mathsf{T}$, one asserts that the sum of square distances of the points y_i to the respective line defined by m_j is minimal.

Clustering of the original data x_i is then performed according to the rule:

Assign x_i to the j-th cluster if the line determined by m_j is the nearest line to y_i

6.3 Hierarchical structure

As mentioned above, rotation of the axes around which the vectors y_i disperse depends on the amount of cluster overlap. For fully disjunctive clusters, provided all eigenvalues are different and the spectral space therefore not rotation invariant, these axes are close to the coordinate axes. For overlapping clusters, where both clusters are expressed to a same extent in the supercluster, the spectral axes are rotated by 45 degrees. In an intermediate case, the axes are rotated by a smaller amount (see Figures 6.1 and 6.2). The axes' rotation stems from the way the point membership to clusters is represented in the eigenvectors. In the eigenvector describing the supercluster, the components corresponding to the points of both subclusters have the same sign, thus stretching the spectral images y_i along a same axis. In the eigenvectors describing the subclusters, the components cor-

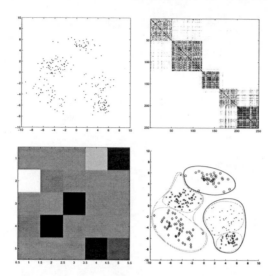

Figure 6.3: Five clusters with partial overlap. **Above left:** scatter plot of the data. **Above right:** Affinity matrix A. **Below left:** Matrix of prototypical vectors M: black $\equiv 1$, white $\equiv -1$. **Below right:** Hierarchically clustered data.

responding to the points of different subclusters have differents sign, distributing y_i's accordingly on the positive and negative side of another coordinate axis.

The axes passing through points y_i are determined by the vectors m_j, which are prototypical spectral vectors for different clusters. So by examining their components, we can obtain information about the hierarchical data structure. Let us construct a matrix M whose columns are the vectors $\mathbf{m}_j$. Now, if any row in the matrix contains large values of a same sign – i.e. components of two prototypical vectors are comparable – this is an indication for a cluster overlap. Clusters described by the columns in which the large values are located form a supercluster. A complementary row also exists, in which the entries of the columns are also large, but with opposite signs. This latter row indicates the splitting of the supercluster into subclusters.

We illustrate this on an example with five clusters, as shown in Figure 6.3. In the second row left is a graphical representation of a matrix M, with dark blocks representing large positive values and white large negative. For demonstration purposes we have ordered the columns of M to reflect our enumeration of the points, so that the first vector in M describes the first cluster, the second vector the second cluster and so on. In the fifth row we see large, positive values at the positions four and five, indicating that the the fourth and the fifth cluster form a supercluster. The first row, with large positive and negative values at the same positions provides for splitting the supercluster. We also notice a less expressed overlap of clusters 1 and 2, indicated by the second and fourth row. Based on these observations, we are able to draw a hierarchical data structure, as shown in the same figure on the right.

6.4 Conductivity-based clustering

We have shown that clustering by spectral analysis works well for block-diagonal-like affinity matrices. We have also argued that the affinity matrix is approximately block-diagonal if we apply the Gaussian kernel on data forming clear clusters. The implicit assumption is that all points in a cluster are relatively close to each other and that the clusters are far away. In other words, the clusters are assumed to be convex, compact and well separated. This description applies to many natural data sets, but other configurations corresponding with the intuitive understanding of clusters are also possible.

A popular example is a ring-like cluster encircling a convex, circular one in the ring center (Figure 6.4). The ring is obviously not convex: the points at the opposite sides of the ring are far from each other, further than from points from the central cluster. Nevertheless, according to our common-sense understanding, we would say that points in the ring form one and the points in the center another cluster. If we compute the affinity matrix of the data, we see that only the central cluster results in a block, whereas the ring cluster produces a diagonal band in the matrix. With a suitable kernel width and sufficient separation of the clusters, the diagonal band is wide. If we are lucky, it approximates a block closely enough for our algorithm to perform correct clustering. This is, however, not the expected data configuration for the algorithm, so it cannot be expected to work well in general.

In order to handle cases where data do not form compact and convex clusters, we have to extend our definition of a cluster. We note that we intuitively regard clusters as continuous concentration of data points, a notion which was applied by Ben-Hur et al. (2001). Two points belong to a cluster if they are close to each other, or if they are well connected by paths of short "hops" over other points. The more such paths exist, the higher the chances are that the points belong to a cluster – an idea somewhat resembling Feynman path integrals.

To quantify cluster membership, we introduce a new affinity measure. Recall the original weighted graph, where edges are assigned larger weights for closer points. Instead of considering two points similar if they are connected by a high-weight edge, we assign them a high affinity if the overall graph conductivity between them is high. This is a complete analogy with electrical networks, where conductivity between two nodes depends not only on the conductivity of the direct path between them, but also on all other indirect paths. Another analogy is with a communication network: we consider edge weights to represent link bandwidths. Then two nodes are well linked if the overall bandwidth over all possible information paths is high.

The conductivity for any two points x_i and x_j is easily computed. We first solve the system of linear equations:

$$G \cdot \varphi = i \tag{6.10}$$

where G is a matrix constructed from the original affinity matrix A:

$$G[p,q] = \begin{cases} \text{for } p = 1 : & \begin{cases} 1 & \text{for } q = 1 \\ 0 & \text{otherwise} \end{cases} \\ \text{otherwise} : & \begin{cases} \sum_{k \neq p} A[p,k] & \text{for } p = q \\ -A[p,q] & \text{otherwise} \end{cases} \end{cases} \tag{6.11}$$

and i is the vector representing points for which the conductivity is computed:

$$i[k] = \begin{cases} -1 & \text{for } k = p \text{ and } p > 1 \\ 1 & \text{for } k = q \\ 0 & \text{otherwise} \end{cases} \tag{6.12}$$

Then the conductivity (link bandwidth) between x_i and x_j, $i < j$ is given by

$$C[i,j] = \frac{1}{\varphi(j) - \varphi(i)} \tag{6.13}$$

which, due to the way i is constructed, can be simplified to

$$C[i,j] = \frac{1}{G^{-1}[i,i] + G^{-1}[j,j] - G^{-1}[i,j] - G^{-1}[j,i]} \tag{6.14}$$

Due to the symmetry, $C[i,j] = C[j,i]$. It therefore suffices to compute G^{-1} only once, in $O(n^3)$ time, and to compute the conductivity matrix C in $O(n^2)$ time.

In electrical engineering, the method above is known as node analysis. To compute the overall conductivity between two nodes i and j in a resistor network, we measure the voltage U_{ij} between them when we let a known current I enter the network at one and leave it at the other node. The overall conductivity is then given by Ohm's law: $G_{ij} = I/U_{ij}$. The voltage is defined as the potential difference between the nodes: $U_{ij} = \varphi_j - \varphi_i$, and the potentials can be computed from Kirchhoff's law, stating that all currents entering a node i must also leave it: $\sum_{j \neq i} I_{ij} = 0$. Applying Ohm's law again, the currents can be expressed over voltages and conductivities, so that this Equation becomes:

$\sum_{j \neq i} G_{ij}U_{ij} = G_{ij}(\varphi_j - \varphi_i) = 0$. Grouping the direct conductivities by the corresponding potentials and formulating the equation for all nodes, we obtain the matrix Equation (6.10). The vector i represents the known current I, which we have transferred to the right side of the equation.

It can be easily seen that in a system of n nodes only $n - 1$ are linearly independent. If we would compose G relying only on Kirchhoff's and Ohm's law, its rows would sum to zero, i.e. the system would be undetermined. In a physical sense, currents entering and leaving $n - 1$ nodes determine also the currents in the n-th node, since they have nowhere else to go. In order to obtain a determined system, we have to choose a node and fix it to a known potential, so it becomes the reference node. In our method we set the potential of the first node to zero ($\varphi_1 = 0$), which is reflected by the way the first rows of G and i are defined in Equations (6.11) and (6.12).

The method here seems to require solving the equations anew for every pair of nodes – the computational analogy of connecting the current source between all pairs of nodes and measuring the voltage. This is, fortunately, not the case: First, since direct conductivities between nodes do not change, it suffices to invert the matrix G only once. And second, for computing the overall conductivity between two nodes, we do not need all voltages in the network, the voltage between these nodes suffices. This allows us to observe only two rows in the G^{-1} matrix. Further, due to the fact that all except two components of vector i are zeros (i.e. the external current source is attached only to two nodes), we only need to consider two columns in G^{-1}. Consequently, the conductivity between any two nodes can be computed from only four elements of the matrix G^{-1}, as the Equation (6.14) shows.

We have left the diagonal elements here undefined. Consequently applying the method above would lead to infinite values, because the denominator in (6.14) is zero for $i = j$. In practical applications, it is a good choice to set them to $\max_{p,q} C[p, q]$. The matrix C then resembles a block-diagonal matrix not only for data forming compact clusters, but also for data whose clusters are best described by high connectivity. We can thus apply our in Section 6.2 described algorithm, using C as the affinity matrix.

Since the matrix C is computed from A, the choice of the kernel width needs some comment. For clustering based on the spectral analysis of A we recommended the kernel width corresponding to the first peak in the distance histogram, or slightly lower. For conductivity-based clustering, where we analyze the spectrum of C, we have experienced that this value is usually too high. Our experiments have shown that the best choice for σ lies at about half the value one would take for analyzing A, i.e. about half of the position of the first peak in the distance histogram, or somewhat below. Otherwise, the algorithm tends to create an over-connected network, thus merging the clusters.

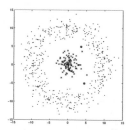 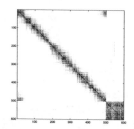

Figure 6.4: Ring and spherical cluster. **Left:** scatter plot of the data. Circles mark misclustered points. **Right:** The affinity matrix A.

6.5 Tests of spectral clustering

Besides toy examples presented so far, we have tested our two algorithms on three hard artificial data sets and on two standard benchmark data sets containing real-world data.

The data set from Figure 6.4 was already mentioned in section 6.4. It consists of a spherical cluster of 100 normally distributed points, encircled by a cluster of 500 points distributed along a ring. The set is considered hard for clustering because clusters are not linearly separable and their centers coincide. Distance-based algorithms working directly in the input space, like K-means, are unable to correctly cluster the data. Our simpler algorithm, using a Gaussian kernel with $\sigma = 2$ as the affinity function, separates the data into the original two clusters with only two misclassifcations. The second algorithm, based on the conductivity matrix, achieves the same result.

In Figure 6.5, an even more complicated data set is shown. Six hundred points are distributed in a 3D-space along two rings in perpendicular planes, intersecting each other. The points are dispersed normally with the standard deviation of 0.1. The data set is harder than the one above because not even one cluster is compact. Both our algorithms perform very well, correctly clustering all points. However, if we increase the dispersion, the simpler algorithm clearly falls behind. For the dispersion of 0.15 it misclassifies 105 points (about one sixth of the data set), and for 0.2 even 149. The conductivity matrix algorithm still performs well, misclassifying only one point in the first and five in the second case (Figure 6.6).

We have also tested the algorithm on a variant of Wieland's two spirals (Figure 6.7). This artificial data set is used as a standard benchmark in supervised learning (see Fahlman, 1988). In Wieland's original set, each spiral consists of 97 points and coils three times around the origin. At the outer ends of the spirals, points from the same spiral are further away than points from different ones — for clus-

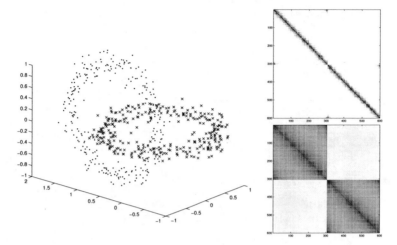

Figure 6.5: Two intersecting ring clusters with data dispersion $\sigma_D = 0.1$. **Left:** scatter plot of the data. **Right above:** Affinity matrix A computed with the Gaussian kernel. **Right below:** Conductivity matrix C.

tering, an extremely unpleasant fact. We used spirals with double point density, resulting in 193 points per spiral. The set is still very inconvenient and even our conductivity matrix is far from being block-diagonal. Nevertheless, with $\sigma = 0.2$ our conductivity-based algorithm achieves the correct clustering for all points.

A classical real-world benchmark is the Iris data set (Fisher, 1936, Murphy and Aha, 1994). It contains 150 measurements, each of four physical dimensions for three sorts of iris flowers. Each of the sorts – setosa, versicolor and virginica – is represented with 50 measurements. This data set is particularly interesting for our algorithm because the latter two classes are not linearly separable and overlap. The overlap is clearly visible in the affinity matrix, where the two last blocks form a larger block. The affinity matrix was computed using a Gaussian kernel with $\sigma = 0.75$, as the distance histogram suggests. Using our simpler algorithm we were able to cluster the data into three clusters, with 10 misclassifications (Figure 6.8). In the prototype vectors' matrix M, graphically represented in Figure 6.8 right, we see that the second and the third entry in the second row are both large, suggesting that the last two clusters form a supercluster. The conductivity matrix algorithm performs equally well. Good results are achieved with $\sigma = 0.375$, for larger kernel widths it easily merges the two overlapping clusters.

The algorithm by Girolami (2002) has been reported to perform better. In ex-

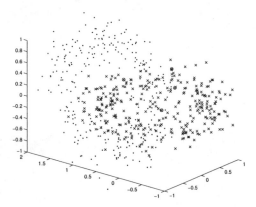

Figure 6.6: Scatter plot of the intersecting ring clusters with dispersion $\sigma_D = 0.2$. Circles mark misclustered points.

periments, the results could be reproduced only occasionally, strongly depending on the initialization. Often, the algorithm performed considerably worse. This is not surprising since the algorithm is stochastic. The algorithm proposed in this chapter is deterministic, using the principal eigenvectors as fixed initialization for the K-lines algorithm.

Another real-world benchmark on which we tested our algorithms is the Wine data set (Murphy and Aha, 1994). Similar to Iris, it contains 178 measurements of 13 different variables concerning wine grapes. With our simpler algorithm we were able to cluster data into three clusters with five misclassifications, and to show that they all form a common supercluster (Figure 6.9). Before processing the data, we scaled them by their standard deviation and used $\sigma = 2.5$ for computing the affinity matrix. The conductivity matrix algorithm, using $\sigma = 1.25$, performs in this case worse, misclassifying 12 points (6.75% of the data set). This is probably due to the high overlap of the clusters, resulting in an unusually high level of connectivity between points, and to the unusually high dimensionality for so little data. The algorithm can be further improved by using a context-dependent similarity measure (Poland and Fischer, 2003).

The algorithm by Ng et al., using K-means for clustering spectral images, performs somewhat worse. Although occasionally reaching only two misclassifications for the data set from Figure 6.4, depending on the initialization it often produces blatantly wrong clustering, with hundreds of misclassified points. For the two intersecting rings from Figure 6.6 it consistently produces six misclassifications and for the Iris data set mostly between eight and sixteen, but occasionally

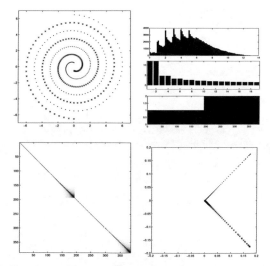

Figure 6.7: Clustering of two spirals. **Above left:** Scatter plot of the data. **Above right:** distance histogram (top); 20 largest eigenvalues (middle) and cluster membership chart (bottom). **Below left:** Conductivity matrix C. **Below right:** Spectral plot along the top two eigenvectors.

over 60. For the Wine set it performs very well, misclassifying only between three and four points. The results are summarized in Table 6.1.

6.6 Spectral Clustering of string data

Since spectral clustering relies only on the affinity matrix, it is easy to apply it to string data. Affinity can be defined over a string distance in the same way as for numerical data. It can also be defined as the string similarity, based on some scoring matrix, like PAM or BLOSUM. The former approach has the advantage of non-linearity, controlled by the kernel width σ, which allows for sharper separation between clusters. The latter can nevertheless be pursued, if σ cannot be deduced in a meaningful way.

Spectral clustering of the garbled English words was performed using the negative Levenshtein distance as the affinity measure. A constant term was added to all affinity values, to achieve a non-negative affinity matrix. This approach avoids manually choosing a parameter, like kernel width. As can be seen from the simi-

Table 6.1: Comparison of algorithms performance on different data sets. The middle column shows the number of misclassified points or, in case of stochastic algorithm, the range of observed misclassifications. The right column shows the same numbers as percentage of the set size.

Algorithm	Absolute error (range)	Relative error (% range)
Iris		
Girolami (reported)	3	2
Girolami (measured)	7 – 15	4.7 – 10
Ng	8 – 69	5.3 – 46
Simple spectral	10	6.7
Conductivity spectral	10	6.7
Wine		
Girolami (measured)	12 – 71	6.7 – 40
Ng	3 – 4	1.7 – 2.2
Simple spectral	5	2.8
Conductivity spectral	12	6.7
Two spirals (double density)		
Girolami (measured)	153 – 193	40 – 50
Ng	174 – 192	45 – 49.8
Simple spectral	192	49.8
Conductivity spectral	0	0

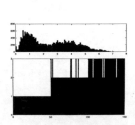
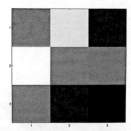

Figure 6.8: Clustering of the Iris data set. **Left:** distance histogram (top); cluster membership chart (bottom). **Right:** Matrix of prototypical vectors M (black $\equiv$ 1, white $\equiv -1$).

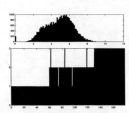
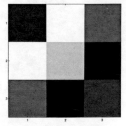

Figure 6.9: Clustering of the Wine data set. **Left:** distance histogram (top); cluster membership chart (bottom). **Right:** Matrix of prototypical vectors M.

larity histogram (Figure 6.10), there is only a small number of possible similarity values, due to the simple and integer distance measure used. It is therefore not obvious from the histogram, which similarity corresponds to data from the same cluster.

For the data generated by 50% noise, seven blocks are clearly visible in the matrix, corresponding to nicely enumerated seven word clusters. For the 75% noisy data, the blocks are not so obvious. In both cases, taking a look at the eigenvalues reveals one big cluster (compare with the Sammon mapping, Figure 3.3). However closing up on the remaining vectors, we note that they continuously fall until the seventh, and then remain largely constant. Performing the K-lines algorithm in the spectral space leads to a quite good assignment of the data to the clusters, even for very noisy data.

For the hemoglobine data, the BLOSUM62-induced distance measure was applied. As affinity function, a Gaussian kernel was used. The first peak in the distance histogram (Figure 6.11) appears somewhere between 200 and 400. Here,

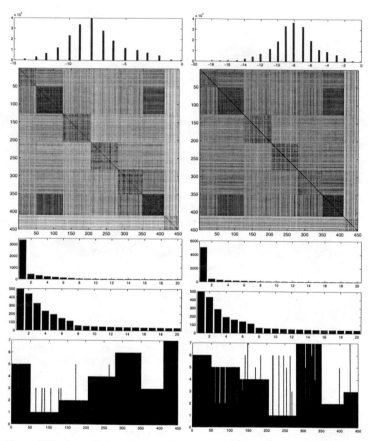

Figure 6.10: Spectral clustering of garbled english words. **Left:** Data generated with 50% noise. **Right:** Data generated with 75% noise. **Both columns, top-down:** similarity (negative distance) histogram; the affinity matrix A; the first 20 eigenvalues; zoom-in into the eigenvalues; predicted cluster memberships.

$\sigma = 300$ was used. In the affinity matrix, two blocks are obvious, and the spectrum contains two high eigenvalues. The algorithm correctly classifies all sequences. However, if we take a closer look at the eigenvalues, we notice that a large drop appears after the fifth eigenvalue. Clustering the data into five clusters splits the first, α cluster into three, and β into two. All but 11 data (some 3%) are correctly classified. The splitting of the data is obvious from the hierarchy matrix M. We notice that large values appear simultaneously in the second and the fifth column, suggesting that clusters 2 and 5 form a supercluster. The same holds for the first, third, and fourth column. A Sammon map of the data, with five classes marked, is shown in Figure 6.12.

Spectral clustering also reveals why the five kinase families are so hard to cluster (Figure 6.13). In the distance histogram, the first peak lies around 2500, but the second is not far away, at about 2800. The data are enumerated in the order: AGC, CaMK, CMGC, PTK, OPK. Looking at the affinity matrix, it can be seen that the first two families are actually subclusters of a larger, compact cluster. Also, in the CMGC family, a number of subclusters can be recognized. The transition between PTK and OPK is gradual, and both share similarities with AGC and CaMK families, PTK less then OPK. In both families, further subclusters are recognizable.

A look at the eigenvalues suggest that there are three big clusters. Clustering the data into three clusters puts the AGC and CaMK families into the first, CMGC into the second, and the large PTK family into the third cluster. The OPK family is split between them. A closer look at the eigenvalues shows another drop after the fifth eigenvalue. Clustering the data into five clusters reconstructs the original families with 47 misclassifications. All but one misclassified sequences are from the OPK group. At an even finer scale, another drop can be seen after the eighth eigenvalue. Clustering the data into eight clusters leaves AGC and CaMK families unchanged, but reveals three subclusters in the CMGC family: the CDK group, a cluster containing the ERK (MAP) and GSK3 groups, and a cluster containing the Casein kinase II and the Clk families. Other CMGC kinases are assigned to the first (CDK) group. Also, the PTK group is divided into two clusters, one of the non-membrane spanning protein-tyrosine kinases and the other of the membrane spanning protein-tyrosine kinases. The OPK family is still not well represented, and sequences are assigned to a separate cluster, to CaMK cluster, and to the last CMGC subcluster.

Phylogenetic trees, mentioned in the Introduction in the context of the kinase data set, are also commonly applied in clustering of string data, especially biological sequences. The trees themselves graphically represent similarities between sequences in a hierarchical manner. The sequences are considered leaves of the binary tree, which is constructed by connecting the similar sequences by branches into nodes, and further connecting similar nodes until all sequences are connected.

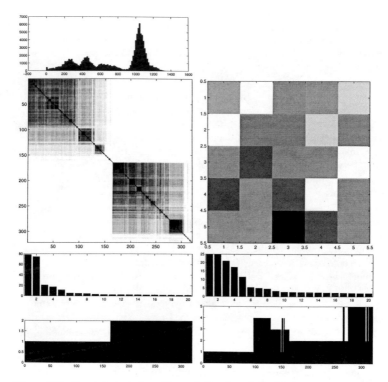

Figure 6.11: Spectral clustering of hemoglobine data. **Left:** Distance histogram (top); Affinity matrix A; Eigenvalues; Cluster membership (bottom). **Right:** Hierarchy matrix M (top); A close-up into the eigenvalues; Cluster membership for five clusters (bottom).

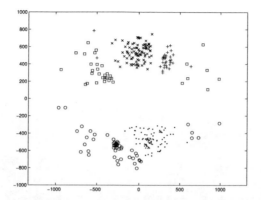

Figure 6.12: Sammon mapping for two hemoglobine chains. Sequences belonging to different subclusters, as discovered by the spectral clustering, are differently marked.

The clustering itself is commonly performed by an expert, who takes not only the sequence similarities into account, but also his knowledge, e.g. about their biological function. Clustering can also be automated, by applying a general agglomerative hierarchical clustering algorithm and cutting the branches when some criterion, like their length (corresponding to the node dissimilarity) is met.

For the presented data set, the result obtained by spectral clustering mostly matches the expert clustering based on the phylogenetic tree (Hanks and Quinn, 1991): AGC and CaMK families are mapped onto nearby branches, close to each other. Inside clusters, long branches – corresponding to a lower similarity – lead to different subclusters of the PTK and CMGC families. The only obvious problem is with the OPK "family", which is not compact and only characterized by belonging to no other family. For successful automated clustering, an algorithm would have to be explicitly designed to support such cases.

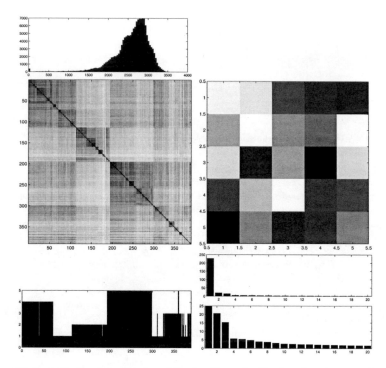

Figure 6.13: Spectral clustering of the five kinase families into five clusters, using $\sigma = 2500$. **Left:** Distance histogram (top); Affinity matrix A; Cluster assignment. **Right:** Hierarchy matrix M of the data (top); First 20 eigenvalues; A close-up into the eigenvalues (bottom).

Chapter 7

Conclusion

The pattern recognition algorithms for strings presented in this thesis have been obtained by defining numerical measures – distance, average, and kernel – for strings and applying them in well-known pattern recognition algorithms for numerical data. Defining numerical measures for strings involves problems not present in numerical data: The computational complexity is much higher, and for computing the average, no efficient algorithm exists, so approximative heuristics must be applied. Even more, since strings are discrete structures, an unambiguous solution does not always exist.

Nevertheless, the experiments show that pattern recognition algorithms can be successfully applied for strings. For simple, usually two-class data sets, Sammon mapping provides already a good insight into the data structure. For complex sets, the mapping dimensionality suitable for visualization is often not powerful enough to capture the structure. More information can be provided by clustering algorithms. Here, the spectral clustering is obviously superior to K-means and SOM and thus the most promising.

For classification, LVQ produces prototypes representing the classes. But, as the experiments show, more prototypes per class normally do not cover the classes uniformly. Instead, one prototype is usually responsible for the largest part of the class, whereas others cover the outliers. If the prototypes themselves are not interesting, but only the classification matters, two other algorithms are a good alternative. Depleted nearest neighbor is simple and fast, and produces the set of boundary prototypes sufficient for classification. However, it is only a heuristics, with no established theoretical properties or performance guarantees. In its simple form it performs the perfect classification of the training set, thus bearing the risk of poor generalization. By setting a training parameter this behavior can be modified, but only indirectly.

More complex and computationally intensive are support vector machines. They are theoretically founded and can be applied to strings by defining the kernel over string similarity or distance. Like depleted nearest neighbor, they produce the set of boundary prototypes – the support vectors – and, in addition, assign a weight to them. Their generalization ability can be directly influenced by the choice of parameters.

Many of the algorithms used in this thesis rely on a distance measure. However, recent developments (Fischer, 2003) show that at least some of them can be defined simply over a similarity measure, thus circumventing some of the problems involved with distance. Algorithms in this thesis were tested on artificial data and data from molecular biology. However, potential application fields for string pattern recognition algorithms are much wider. One field, speech recognition, has already been mentioned in the Introduction. Also, various applications in social sciences are imaginable. For instance, one could code sequential behavior steps as a string of symbols, each representing a step. An example of such steps would be: seeing an advertisement, inquiring about the product, visiting the manufacturers web site, seeing someone having the product, buying the product, and so on. Analyzing the sequences of a large set of people could help companies optimize their marketing strategies. Numerous other examples can also be given. It can be therefore expected that pattern recognition for symbol strings will be intensively applied in the future.

Bibliography

D.K. Agrafiotis. A new method for analyzing protein sequence relationships based on Sammon maps. *Protein Science*, 6(2):287–293, June 1997.

S. F. Altschul and D. J. Lipman. Trees, stars, and multiple biological sequence alignment. *SIAM Journal of Applied Mathematics*, 49(1):197–209, 1989.

S.F. Altschul, W. Gish, W. Miller, E.W. Meyers, and D.J. Lipman. Basic local alignment search tool. *Journal of Molecular Biology*, 215:403–410, 1990.

I. Apostol and W. Szpankowski. Indexing and mapping of proteins using a modified nonlinear Sammon projection. *Journal of Computational Chemistry*, June 1999.

W.C. Barker, J.S. Garavelli, D.H. Haft, L.T. Hunt, C.R. Marzec, B.C. Orcutt, G.Y. Srinivasarao, L.-S.L. Yeh, R.S. Ledley, H.-W. Mewes, F. Pfeiffer, and A. Tsugita. The PIR-international protein sequence database. *Nucleic Acids Research*, 26(1):27–32, 1998.

H. Bauer and K. Pawelzik. Quantifying the neighborhood preservation of self-organizing feature maps. *IEEE Transactions on Neural Networks*, 3:570–579, 1992.

A. Ben-Hur, D. Horn, H.T. Siegelmann, and V. Vapnik. A support vector method for clustering. In T.K. Leen, T.G. Dietterich, and V. Tresp, editors, *Advances in Neural Information Processing Systems 13*, pages 367–373. MIT Press, 2001.

C.M. Bishop. *Neural Networks for Pattern Recognition*. Oxford University Press, 1995.

J. Buhmann. Stochastic algorithms for exploratory data analysis: Data clustering and data visualization. In Michael I. Jordan, editor, *Learning in Graphical Models*, pages 405–419. MIT Press, Cambridge, MA, 1999.

W.M. Campbell. A sequence kernel and its application to speaker recognition. In T.G. Dietterich, S. Becker, and Z. Ghahramani, editors, *Advances in Neural*

Information Processing Systems 14, pages 1157–1163, Cambridge, MA, 2002. MIT Press.

T.M. Cover and P.E. Hart. Nearest neighbor pattern classification. *IEEE Transactions on Information Theory*, IT-13(1):21–27, 1967.

N. Cristianini and J. Shawe-Taylor. *An Introduction to Support Vector Machines*. Cambridge University Press, Cambridg, 2000.

N. Cristianini, J. Shawe-Taylor, and J. Kandola. Spectral kernel methods for clustering. In T.G. Dietterich, S. Becker, and Z. Ghahramani, editors, *Advances in Neural Information Processing Systems 14*, pages 649–655, Cambridge, MA, 2002. MIT Press.

M.O. Dayhoff, R.M. Schwartz, and B.C. Orcutt. A model of evolutionary change in proteins. In M.O. Dayhoff, editor, *Atlas of Protein Sequence and Structure*, volume 5, pages 345–352, Washington, DC., 1978. Natl. Biomed. Res. Found.

R.O. Duda, P.E. Hart, and D.G. Stork. *Pattern Classification*. John Wiley & Sons, Inc., New York, 2001.

E. Erwin, K. Obermayer, and K. Schulten. Self-organizing maps: Ordering, convergence properties and energy functions. *Biological Cybernetics*, 67:47–55, 1992.

S.E. Fahlman. Faster-learning variations on back-propagation: An empirical study. In David Touretzky, Geoffrey Hinton, and Terrence Sejnowski, editors, *Proceedings of the 1988 Connectionist Models Summer School*, pages 38–51, San Mateo, CA, USA, 1988. Morgan Kaufmann.

J. Felsenstein. Numerical methods for inferring the evolutionary trees. *The Quarterly Review of Biology*, 57(4):379–404, 1982.

I. Fischer. Similarity-preserving metrics for amino-acid sequences. In *The 22nd GIF Meeting on Challenges in Genomic Research: Neurogenerative Diseases, Stem Cells, Bioethics*, pages 30–31, Heidelberg, July 2002. German-Israeli Foundation for Scientific Research and Development.

I. Fischer. Similarity-based neural networks for applications in computational molecular biology. In *Proceedings of The 5th International Symposium on Intelligent Data Analysis*, Berlin, 2003. Accepted for publication.

I. Fischer and J. Poland. An analysis of spectral clustering, affinity functions and hierarchy. *Journal of Machine Learning Research*, submitted, 2003.

I. Fischer, S. Wiest, and A. Zell. An example of generating internet-based course material. In D. Kalpić and V. Dobrić, editors, *Proceedings of the 22nd Intl. Conf. Information Technology Interfaces ITI 2000*, pages 229–234, Pula, Croatia, June 2000.

I. Fischer and A. Zell. Processing symbolic data with self-organizing maps. In Hans-Joachim Böhme Horst-Michael Groß, Klaus Debes, editor, *Workshop SOAVE '2000*, number 643 in 10, pages 96–105, Düsseldorf, 2000a. VDI Verlag.

I. Fischer and A. Zell. String averages and self-organizing maps for strings. In H. Bothe and R. Rojas, editors, *Proceedings of the Neural Computation 2000*, pages 208–215, Canada / Switzerland, May 2000b. ICSC Academic Press.

I. Fischer and A. Zell. Visualization of neural networks using java applets. In M. Hoffmann, editor, *"Innovations in Education for Electrical and Information Engineering (EIE)", Proceedings of the 11th annual conference of the EAEEIE*, pages 71–76, Ulm, April 2000c. Universität Ulm, Abteilung Mikrowellentechnik.

R.A. Fisher. The use of multiple measurements in taxonomic problems. *Annual Eugenics*, 7, Part II:179–188, 1936.

R. Fletcher and C.M. Reeves. Function minimization by conjugate gradients. *Computer Journal*, 7:149–154, 1964.

M. Friedman and A. Kandel. *Introduction to Pattern Recognition*. Imperial College Press, London, 1999.

B. Fritzke. *Vektorbasierte Neuronale Netze*. Shaker Verlag, Aachen, Germany, 1998.

M.R. Garey and D.S. Johnson. *Computers and Intractability*. Freeman, San Francisco, 1979.

G.W. Gates. The reduced nearest neighbor rule. *IEEE Transactions on Information Theory*, IT-18:431–433, May 1974.

M. Girolami. Mercer kernel-based clustering in feature space. *IEEE Transactions on Neural Networks*, 13(3):780–784, May 2002. URL *http://cis.paisley.ac.uk/giro-ci0/pubs_2001/mnl0049_df.zip*.

K.C. Gowda and G. Krishna. The condensed nearest-neighbor rule using the concept of mutual nearest neighborhood. *IEEE Transactions on Information Theory*, IT-25(4):488–490, July 1979.

D. Gusfield. Efficient methods for multiple sequence alignment with guaranteed error bounds. *Bulletin of Mathematical Biology*, 55(1):141–154, 1993.

D. Gusfield. *Algorithms on Strings, Trees, and Sequences*. Cambridge University Press, 1997.

S. Hanks and A.M. Quinn. Protein kinase catalytic domain sequence database: Identification of conserved features of primary structure and classification of family members. *Methods in Enzymology*, 200:38–62, 1991.

S.K. Hanks and T. Hunter. The eukaryotic protein kinase superfamily: kinase (catalytic) domain structure and classification. *FASEB Journal*, 9:576–596, 1995.

P.E. Hart. The condensed nearest neighbor rule. *IEEE Transactions on Information Theory*, IT-4:515–516, May 1968.

A. Hatzis, P. Green, and S. Howard. Optical logo-therapy - (OLT). A computer based speech training system for the visualisation of articulation using connectionist techniques. In *Proc. IOA.*, pages 299–306., 1996. URL *http://citeseer.nj.nec.com/hatzis96optical.html*.

D.O. Hebb. The first stage of perception: growth of an assembly. In *The Organization of Behaviour*, chapter 4 and Introduction, pages xi–xix, 60–78. Wiley, New York, 1949.

R. Hecht-Nielsen. Counterpropagation networks. In M. Caudill and C. Butler, editors, *Proceedings of the IEEE First Conference on Neural Networks*, volume 2, pages 19–32. IEEE, 1987.

S. Henikoff and J.G. Henikoff. Amino acid substitution matrices from protein blocks. In *Proceedings of the National Academy of Sciences*, volume 89, pages 10915–10919, Washington, DC, November 1992.

T. Heskes. Energy functions for self-organizing maps. In S. Oja, E. & Kaski, editor, *Kohonen Maps*, pages 303–316. Elsevier, Amsterdam, 1999. URL *http://citeseer.nj.nec.com/heskes99energy.html*.

D. Hirshberg. A linear space algorith for computing maximal common subsequences. *Communications of the ACM*, 18:341–343, 1975.

T. Jaakkola and D. Haussler. Exploiting generative models in discriminative classifiers. In M.S. Kearns, S.A. Solla, and D.A. Cohn, editors, *Advances in Neural Information Processing Systems 11*, Cambridge, MA, 1998. MIT Press.

J. Kececioglu. The maximum weight trace problem in multiple sequence alignment. In *Proceedings of the Fourth Symposium on Combinatorial Pattern Matching*, volume 684 of *Lecture Notes in Computer Science*, pages 106–119, Berlin, 1993. Springer.

T. Kohonen. Self-organized formation of topologically correct feature maps. *Biological Cybernetics*, 43:59–69, 1982.

T. Kohonen. Median strings. *Pattern Recognition Letters*, 3:309–313, 1985.

T. Kohonen. An introduction to neural computing. *Neural Networks*, 1:3–16, 1988a.

T. Kohonen. Learning vector quantization. *Neural Networks*, 1, Suplement 1:303, 1988b.

T. Kohonen. Improved versions of learning vector quantization. In *Proceedings of the International Joint Conference on Neural Networks*, volume 1, pages 545–550, San Diego, June 1990. IEEE.

T. Kohonen. *Self-Organizing Maps*. Springer, Berlin Heidelberg, 1995.

T. Kohonen, J. Hynninen, J. Kangas, and J. Laaksonen. SOM_PAK: The Self-Organizing Map program package. Report A31, Helsinki University of Technology, Laboratory of Computer and Information Science, 1 1996. URL *http://-www.cis.hut.fi/research/som_lvq_pak.shtml*.

T. Kohonen and P. Somervuo. Self-organizing maps of symbol strings. *Neurocomputing*, 21:19–30, 1998.

U.H.-G. Kreßel. Pairwise clustering and support vector machines. In Bernhard Schölkopf, Christoper J.C. Burges, and Alexander J. Smola, editors, *Advances in Kernel Methods*, pages 255–268. MIT Press, 1999.

J.B. Kruskal and D. Sankoff. An antology of algorithms and concepts for sequence comparison. In David Sankoff and Joseph B. Kruskal, editors, *Time Warps, String Edits, and Macromolecules: the Theory and Practice of Sequence Comparison*, Reading, MA, 1983. Addison-Wesley.

J.A. Lee, A. Lendasse, N. Doneckers, and M. Verleysen. A robust nonlinear projection method. In *ESANN'2000 Proceedings - European Symposium on Artificial Neural Networks*, pages 13–20. D-Facto public., 2000. ISBN 2-930307-00-5.

C. Leslie, E. Eskin, and W.S. Noble. The spectrum kernel: A string kernel for SVM protein classification. In *Pacific Symposium on Biocomputing*, volume 7, pages 566–575, January 2002. URL *http://www.smi.stanford.edu/projects/-helix/psb02/leslie.pdf*.

L.I. Levenshtein. Binary codes capable of correcting deletions, insertions, and reversals. *Soviet Physics–Doklady*, 10(7):707–710, 1966.

S.P. Lloyd. Least squares quantization in PCM. *IEEE Transactions on Information Theory*, 28(2):129–137, 1982.

H. Lodhi, J. Shawe-Taylor, N. Cristianini, and C. Watkins. Text classification using string kernels. Technical report NC-TR-2000-79, NeuroCOLT2, June 2000. URL *http://www.neurocolt.com/tech_reps/2000/00079.ps.gz*.

J. MacQueen. Some methods for classification and analysis of multivariate data. In L. M. Le Cam and J. Neyman, editors, *Proceedings of the 5th Berkeley Symposium on Mathematical Statistics and Probability*, volume 1, pages 281–297, Berkeley and Los Angeles, 1967. University of California Press.

W.J. Masek and M.S. Paterson. A faster algorithm computing string edit distance. *Journal of Computer and System Sciences*, 20:18–31, 1980.

W.J. Masek and M.S. Paterson. How to compute string-edit distances quickly. In David Sankoff and Joseph B. Kruskal, editors, *Time Warps, String Edits, and Macromolecules: the Theory and Practice of Sequence Comparison*, pages 337–349. Addison-Wesley, Reading, MA, 1983.

W.S. McCulloch and W. Pitts. A logical calculus of the ideas immanent in nervous activity. *Bulletin of Mathematical Biophysics*, 5:115–133, 1943.

M. Meilă and J. Shi. Learning segmentation by random walks. In T.K. Leen, T.G. Dietterich, and V. Tresp, editors, *Advances in Neural Information Processing Systems 13*, pages 873–879. MIT Press, 2001.

T.M. Mitchell. *Machine Learning*. McGraw-Hill, New York, 1997.

J.J. More. The Levenberg-Marquardt algorithm: Implementation and theory. In A. Watson, editor, *Numerical Analysis*, Lecture Notes in Mathematics 630, pages 105–116. Springer, Berlin Heidelberg, 1977.

P.M. Murphy and D.W. Aha. UCI repository of machine learning databases, 1994. URL *http://www.ics.uci.edu/~mlearn/MLRepository.html*.

F. Murtagh. Multivariate data analysis software and resources page, 1992. URL *http://astro.u-strasbg.fr/˜fmurtagh/mda-sw/*.

S.B. Needleman and C.C. Wunsch. A general method applicable to the search for similarities in the amin acid sequence of two proteins. *Journal of Molecular Biology*, 48:443–453, 1970.

A.Y. Ng, M.I. Jordan, and Y. Weiss. On spectral clustering: Analysis and an algorithm. In T.G. Dietterich, S. Becker, and Z. Ghahramani, editors, *Advances in Neural Information Processing Systems 14*, Cambridge, MA, 2002. MIT Press.

K. Pearson. Mathematical contributions to the theory of evolution. iii. regression, heredity and panmixia. *Philosophical Transactions of the Royal Society of London*, 187:253–318, 1896.

W. R. Pearson and D. J. Lipman. Improved tools for biological sequence comparison. In *Proceedings of the National Academy of Sciences of the U.S.A*, volume 85, pages 2444–2448, Washington, DC, 4 1988. National Academy of Sciences of the U.S.A.

E. Pekalska, D. De Ridder, R.P.W. Duin, and M.A. Kraaijveld. A new method of generalizing Sammon mapping with application to algorithm speed-up. In M. Boasson, J.A. Kaandorp, J.F.M Tonino, and M.G. Vosselman, editors, *Proceedings ASCI'99, 5th Annual Conference of the Advanced School for Computing and Imaging the National Academy of Sciences*, pages 221–228, ASCI, Delft, The Netherlands, June 1999. URL *http://www.ph.tn.tudelft.nl/-Research/neural/feature_extraction/papers/asci99b.html*.

P. Perona and W. Freeman. A factorization approach to grouping. *Lecture Notes in Computer Science*, 1406:655–670, 1998. URL *http://citeseer.nj.nec.com/-perona98factorization.html*.

W. Pitts and W.S. McCulloch. How we know universals: the perception of auditory and visual forms. *Bulletin of Mathematical Biophysics*, 9:127–147, 1947.

J. Poland and I. Fischer. Robust clustering based on context-dependent similarity. *Journal of Machine Learning Research*, submitted, 2003.

M. Riedmiller and H. Braun. A direct adaptive method for faster backpropagation learning: The RPROP algorithm. In *Proceedings of the IEEE International Conference on Neural Networks (ICNN 93)*. IEEE, 1993.

H. Ritter, T. Martinez, and K. Schulten. *Neuronale Netze: Eine Einführung in die Neuroinformatik Selbstorganisierender Netzwerke*. Addison Wesley, 1990.

F. Rosenblatt. The perceptron: a probabilistic model for information storage and organization in the brain. *Psychological Review*, 65:386–408, 1958.

J.W. Sammon, Jr. A nonlinear mapping for data structure analysis. *IEEE Transactions on Computers*, 18(5):401–409, 1969.

D. Sankoff and J.B. Kruskal. *Time Warps, String Edits, and Macromolecules: the Theory and Practice of Sequence Comparison*. Addison-Wesley, Reading, MA, 1983.

B. Schölkopf. *Support Vector Learning. PhD Thesis*. Oldenbourg Verlag, Munich, Germany, 1997. URL *http://svm.first.gmd.de/papers/book_ref.ps.gz*.

B. Schölkopf, J. Platt, J. Shawe-Taylor, A. J. Smola, and R. C. Williamson. Estimating the support of a high-dimensional distribution. Technical Report 99–87, Microsoft Research, 1999. URL *http://www.kernel-machines.org/papers/-oneclass-tr.ps.gz*.

J.C. Setubal and J. Meidanis. *Intorduction to Computational Molecular Biology*. PWS Publishing Company, Boston, 1997.

J. Shi and J. Malik. Normalized cuts and image segmentation. *IEEE Transactions on Pattern Analysis and Machine Intelligence*, 22(8):888–905, 2000. URL *http://citeseer.nj.nec.com/shi97normalized.html*.

H. Shimodaira, K.-I. Noma, M. Nakai, and S. Sagayama. Dynamic time-alignment kernel in support vector machine. In T.G. Dietterich, S. Becker, and Z. Ghahramani, editors, *Advances in Neural Information Processing Systems 14*, pages 921–928, Cambridge, MA, 2002. MIT Press.

J.W. Smith, J.E. Everhart, W.C. Dickson, W.C. Knowler, and R.S. Johannes. Using the ADAP learning algorithm to forecast the onset of diabetes mellitus. In *Proceedings of the Symposium on Computer Applications and Medical Care*, pages 261–265. IEEE Computer Society Press, 1988.

C.W. Swonger. Sample set condensation for a condenset nearest neighbor decision rule for pattern recognition. In S. Watanabe, editor, *Frontiers in Pattern Recognition*, pages 511–526. Academic Press, New York, 1972.

D. Tax. *One-class classification. Ph.D. Thesis*. University of Delft, 2001. URL *http://www.ph.tn.tudelft.nl/~davidt/thesis.pdf*.

I. Tomek. Two modifications of CNN. *IEEE Transactions on Systems, Man and Cybernetics*, SMC-6:769–772, November 1976.

E. Ukkonen. Algorithms for approximate string matching. *Information and Control*, 64:100–118, 1985.

W. N. Venables and B. D. Ripley. Modern applied statistics with S-PLUS; R versions of software, 2001. URL *http://www.stats.ox.ac.uk/pub/MASS3/*.

J.-P. Vert. Support vector machine prediction of signal peptide cleavage site using a new class of kernels for strings. In *Pacific Symposium on Biocomputing*, volume 7, pages 649–660, January 2002.

T. Villmann, R. Der, and T. Martinetz. Topology preservation in self-organizing feature maps: Exact definition and measurment. *IEEE Transactions on Neural Networks*, 8:256–266, 1997.

R.A. Wagner and M. J. Fischer. The string to string correction problem. *Journal of the ACM*, 21:168–173, 1974.

L. Wang and T. Jiang. On the complexity of multiple sequence alignment. *Journal of Computational Biology*, 1(4):337–348, 1994.

C. Watkins. Dynamic alignment kernels. Technical report CSD-TR-98-11, Royal Holloway University of London, Department of Computer Science, Egham, Surrey TW20 0EX, England, January 1999. URL *http://www.cs.rhul.ac.uk/home/chrisw/dynk.ps.gz*.

Y. Weiss. Segmentation using eigenvectors: A unifying view. In *ICCV (2)*, pages 975–982, 1999. URL *http://citeseer.nj.nec.com/weiss99segmentation.html*.

B. Widrow and M.E. Hoff. Adaptive switching circuits. In *IRE WESCON Convention Record*, pages 96–104, New York, 1960. IRE.

C.K. Wong and A.K. Chandra. Bounds for the string matching problem. *Journal of the Association for Computer Machinery*, 23:13–16, 1976.